A_Short_History_Of_Mercantilism

A SHORT HISTORY
OF MERCANTILISM

BY

J. W. HORROCKS
M.A., D.Lit.

METHUEN & CO. LTD.
36 ESSEX STREET W.C.
LONDON

First Published in 1925

PRINTED IN GREAT BRITAIN

PREFACE

THIS little book is rather a compendium of the whole subject than an attempt specially to elucidate any particular phase of it. Any originality it may claim is rather in the design and plan than in the matter presented, and the writer here acknowledges his large debt to the researches of others, even where he cannot accept their conclusions.

CONTENTS

vii

A SHORT HISTORY OF MERCANTILISM

CHAPTER I

INTRODUCTION

THE object of this volume is to give an historical account of that regime whereby the State, in different countries, has sought to control economic life in the interests of political and national strength and independence, and which by virtue of the importance that it has attached to the maintenance of a favourable money balance on foreign trade has been called the Mercantile System or Mercantilism. The subject includes, in the first place, an aim of political and national power; in the second, certain ideas as to the true foundations of that power; and in the third, certain methods adopted by the State for the promotion and regulation of agriculture, industry, and commerce to the end of securing and enlarging those foundations.[1]

The term " Mercantile System " is not a satisfactory one. It does not accurately describe or even aptly suggest the essential nature of the complex of theory and practice which it is used to designate. It has been criticized as implying at once too much and too little. The policy, we are told, has never assumed the coherence of a definite system, but has appeared rather as a more or less powerful tendency, or group of tendencies, or as a collection of opportunist expedients. Moreover, it cannot be regarded as a typical expression of the mercantile spirit, which is by no means necessarily inclined to favour a policy of State direction or to connect itself with an ideal of political and national strength and independence. Again, the feature that gave rise to the name was, it is said, only an incidental result of the teaching of its advocates, and the epithet " mercantile " is altogether inadequate to indicate either the range or the purpose of the regime which it is intended to denote.

But, on the other hand, it must be stated that what is known, in the broad yet specific sense which is here followed, as Mercantilism, has always had much the same general aim ; it has always rested upon much the same general principles, though one or other of these has been neglected or specially emphasized in different periods and in different countries ; and whilst there has been an adaptive variation of means, these have always shown a strong family resemblance, by reason of their relation to the general aim and principles. Hence we may fitly speak of the policy as a " system," on the understanding that the word is not to be taken as pointing to a rigid, undeveloping body of rules and practices.

Further, though the adjective " mercantile " has been challenged, no appropriate word has been put forward to occupy its place. The alternative " commercial " is open to a like objection.[2] " Industrial

System," a name used by the classical economists, the followers of Adam Smith, as a label for their own ideas, was declared by their German critic, Frederic List, to be rather applicable to the so-called " Mercantile System," on the ground that the sole purpose of that policy was the establishment of a national industry, whereas the system of " values of exchange " preached by Adam Smith and his disciples underrated the value of a national manufacturing power, and was in truth the " strictest and most consistent mercantile system."[3] But this opinion was based partly upon a rather selective interpretation of Mercantilism and partly upon a failure to appreciate the bearing of Smith's teaching upon home industry, and the transposition of titles would be no real improvement in nomenclature. " Restrictive System," a term sometimes adopted, stresses only the negative aspect of the policy, and to style it " Colbertism," after one of its most famous practitioners,[4] is rather to obscure the historical stretch and significance of the subject. Mercantilism is a regime of economic nationalism, but a nationalist system need not include some of the distinctive features of historic Mercantilism. List calls his own scheme of economy the " National System " ; but whilst he sets forth what he holds to be the merits of the " so-called " Mercantile System, he also draws attention to what he considers to be its defects, and his national economy is one in which mercantilist expedients have only a temporary, provisional, and conditional place, though his teaching has been influential mainly in its mercantilist elements. In the absence of a satisfactory, recognized substitute, therefore, the familiar name is retained as a convenient term for the matter in hand.

The study of Mercantilism is really that of the history of modern civilization from a special point of view—of what has been a common and recurring phase in the political and economic evolution of modern nations and States. Mercantilism has presented an almost invariable association with the growth of national self-consciousness and egotism. It has stood for national power as a necessity for defence and offence, as something to which the economic interests of the people must be subordinated and which they must be made to subserve, and which in its turn must be used to safeguard and advance those interests as distinct from, and even opposed to, those of other peoples. It has stood for economic nationalism or patriotism of the exclusive and aggressive types, and wherever the ruling spirit, whether in absolutist or in constitutional governments, has possessed these qualities, the economic policy which it has prompted has tended to follow what may be described as characteristically mercantilist lines.

A complete elucidation of the subject would trace the development of the ideas, institutions, and conditions which contributed to the formation of mercantilist theory and practice ; it would relate the history of the course of mercantilist policy and its variations in different countries, the effect upon it of racial, social, and geographical diversities, and its influence both in the domestic and in the international spheres, especially in the alternations of peace and war ; and it would notice the mercantilist elements in theories and regimes which have abandoned some but retained other features of the system. Such a survey, in its fullness, is of course not attempted in the present essay. Indeed, we may doubt whether it would be possible in the present state of historical knowledge. The investigation of politico-economic ideas and conditions over the long period and in the many regions involved has not yet attained to such undoubted results as would supply the necessary data for an adequate treatment of the subject in all its bearings. The field which it covers bristles with vexed questions and unsettled matters of fact. The dispute over the name is but a faint reflection of differences about the thing itself. There is division of opinion as to when Mercantilism or the mercantilist tendency first appeared in this country or that ; as to the extent to which it has prevailed and its results in different countries and periods ; as to whether or how far this or that theorist, ruler, or statesman is to be counted in the ranks of the mercantilists ; and, finally, as to how far, on theoretical or historical grounds, the system is to be justified or condemned. With the progress of research and the advance of knowledge, generalization on some of the topics that must be treated or touched upon has become much more difficult. In the sketch which is here presented, general statements perforce bulk largely ; but where these are made without qualification, it is not without a consciousness of modifications or exceptions that might have to be noted if a more detailed handling of the subject were being undertaken. The relevant history of only a few leading countries can be considered at any length, and English and British history is given the main and central prominence in the survey, partly because any common tendency of the spirit of nationalism, as of other impelling forces, can be best apprehended from the shape which it has assumed in one's own land, and partly because, independently of that general consideration, from the history of no other country is there to be obtained so clear an understanding of the Mercantile System, in the successive stages of rise and growth, decline and fall, as that which the British record renders possible.[5]

But the subject, even in its English or British reference, is far from being of merely historical interest. It has an important bearing upon the problems that confront us in the present.   Indeed, the very strength of that bearing makes it hard to interpret the past in this connexion with becoming impartiality.   Its study brings up questions which are so related, in reality or appearance or both, to topics that have been hotly debated in recent times, and which are still in controversy, that the danger of anachronism, against which we have to guard in all historical estimates, besets us with peculiar potency in the attempt at a survey and conclusions here.   Thus a Free Trader of to-day may fail to give due weight to the conditions in which Mercantilism arose, and which influenced its manifestations ; and his opponent may be tempted, by a spirit which has in it something akin to that of the old mercantilist regime, to draw upon some of its methods for suggestions of policy in an environment with which they do not harmonize.

The relevance of the subject in the present is, however, not simply by way of lesson or warning from the historic past. Mercantilism has often been discussed as if it were a phase of politico-economic history practically completed about a hundred years ago. But on the wider view which we are taking, the matter for consideration is to be found extending right down to our own times, which have witnessed, and do witness, mercantilist policy in action, whether on the old lines, as in Japan, where the main features of Elizabethan national economy have been reproduced, or in new adjustments and adaptations, as amongst the western powers. The term " World Economy " is frequently applied to the state of things brought about and represented by the improvements in production, transportation, and communication, the expansion, material and geographical, of the scope of commerce, the extension of capitalist enterprise across political frontiers, and the growth of international arrangements affecting economic interests, which have marked the age of steam and electricity. But this so-called " World Economy " has not been something which has superseded national economies, though it has necessarily conditioned their operation. The economic unit of authority is still the nation or nation State. Moreover, simultaneously with the tendency towards economic internationalism within certain limits, there was developed, out of the policy of protection which was the nineteenth-century offspring of the old Mercantilism, a new Mercantilism which, whilst deriving much of its character from the conditions of the growing "World Economy," ran counter to it, and was largely responsible for the international friction which issued in the great World War.

Britain long ago discarded the Mercantile System, and she continued to practise the principles of Free Trade while the aforesaid movement was in progress in other countries ; but the challenge to her industrial supremacy which came, towards the close of the nineteenth century, from the United States and Germany, combined with other causes to provoke a vigorous campaign on behalf of a drastic change in her fiscal policy. The Tariff Reform propaganda of Mr. Chamberlain drew support from a mixture of old mercantilist ideas with a new imperial spirit. The former Mercantilism had involved the subordination of the interests of the colonies to those of the mother country. But revolution and constitutional advance had utterly transformed the situation in that regard. Indeed, the self-governing colonies had themselves set up national economies which presented some of the essential features of the mercantilist regime, and were even coming to repudiate the term " colony " as applied to them, on the ground that it contained an implication of inferiority. The Tariff Reformers, taking account of these developments, put forward proposals in which were associated, with some inconsistency, the ideas of the economic unity and self-sufficiency of the Empire, the protection of the national unit, imperial preference, and tariff-retaliation for the purpose of forcing better terms for the admission of British products into foreign markets. The campaign made little headway during the years of peace, and in the World War, itself largely the outcome of mercantilist aggression, the myth of the ruin wrought by " one-sided Free Trade " was strikingly exposed. The interdependence of the nations was written in blood as the outstanding lesson of the struggle. Yet Mercantilism, as was to be expected, found something of a market in the shock of war. State control suddenly sprang into the ascendant. Imperial union for military require- ments brought in its train the acceptance of the principle of imperial preference which had been the main plank in Mr. Chamberlain's platform. Since the cessation of hostilities, and especially since the collapse of the boom which followed the Armistice, there has been a recrudescence of apprehensive nationalism which has borne strong traces of the mer- cantilist temper. In countries already protectionist, something in the nature of a panic increase of tariffs has taken place, whilst nations newly organized have hastened to set up tariff walls. In Britain the mer- cantilist notion of self-sufficiency received expres- sion in legislation for the safeguarding of key and other industries, and more recently there has been a renewed Tariff Reform campaign. But these pro- ceedings have done little to obscure the truth that the war has imposed upon national economies the necessity of a new orientation. It is in the sense of international solidarity, which has found partial expression in the covenant of the present League of Nations, that the safeguard of the future must lie. This is fundamentally opposed to that employment of the machinery of State on behalf of an exclusive economic nationalism or imperialism which is of the essence of Mercantilism old or new, and it points rather to the ultimate emergence of a real World Economy, wherein national economies shall be subordinated to the ruling spirit of interdependence as interpreted by international agreement.

CHAPTER II

ANCIENT MERCANTILISM

THE continuous history of Mercantilism, which is our leading theme, belongs to the centuries during which the rise and development of modern nations and States have proceeded along with those of modern money and credit economies, and the factors which contributed to its establishment must be sought chiefly in the stages whereby mediaeval led up to and passed into modern civilization. But something of the informing spirit of Mercantilism, some of its characteristic ideas, and certain of the practical expedients in which it has found concrete expression are undoubtedly to be traced in the politico-economic life of the ancient world. Indeed, mercantilist or semi-mercantilist explanations have been offered for some of the most prominent facts and phases of Greek and Roman history. These, however, have not altogether escaped the danger of anachronism, in the shape of a tendency to put upon the evidence too modern an interpretation, and to fill up the gaps, without due warrant, by suggestions from modern times. Moreover, after the break-up of the old order in the west, we are concerned, in the sphere of politico-economic tendencies and processes, rather with an evolution from new beginnings than with the progress of movements already far advanced, and as our main business is with the fashion of economy which after many centuries resulted from that evolution, it is unnecessary to notice more than briefly such appearances of Mercantilism as are to be observed in the politico-economic systems of antiquity.

We know that money arose and played an important part in the economy of ancient societies, and the quasi-mercantilist opinion which regards the precious metals, whether coined or uncoined, as the pre-eminent form of wealth was widely entertained and had its effect upon public policy.   The notion of the self-sufficing State was a familiar conception, its control over the economic as over other departments of individual and social activity was an accepted commonplace, and in communities where commercial enterprise prevailed the machinery of the State was freely applied both in its support and in order to secure its contribution to the revenue.   Ideas which were to be linked together in the Mercantile System are to be discovered in both Greek and Latin authors, and measures and modes of procedure such as were to have that association are to be found amongst the public acts of Greece, of Rome, of Carthage.   But the conditions which produced them were not adequate, were not sufficiently of the kind, to give them a consistent mercantilist development, to cause them to be drawn together in a definite mercantilist regime.   The will to power and the paternal authority and paramount control of the State were amply asserted, but they failed generally to attain to that specialized regulation of economic life in the interests of political strength and that specialized employment of political power for the increase of the economic resources of the State which, apart from the precise methods adopted, are the distinguishing marks of the Mercantile System. The ancient city States certainly experienced a feeling after Mercantilism, more notably in some cases than in others, but it was never worked out in a coherent and comprehensive mercantilist programme.[1]

There are those who see Mercantilism, not in the full technical sense, but rather as connoting the general spirit of commercial monopoly and expansion, writ large over the development of the ancient world, and who find in it the master-key to the State rivalries and conflicts of classical antiquity. Thus the Peloponnesian War, which engaged the pen of the greatest of historians, figures in this view, though not in the pages of Thucydides himself, as but the military phase of an old commercial struggle, the outcome of an Athenian aggressiveness which was concerned entirely with the acquisition and control of corn supplies, trade routes, markets, and the like ; [2] and the manner in which governments placed their diplomacy and their armies at the service of commerce in the late or Hellenistic period of Greek history has been especially emphasized.[3] Again, Carthage is looked upon as notoriously a State whose policy, equally in peace and in war, was dictated purely by mercantile ambition. It was apparently the one object of her statesmen to win and exploit markets and reserve for her the exclusive advantages of a vast commercial domain. The economic interests of her colonies were ruthlessly subordinated to those of the metropolis, and, in particular, traffic on their part with the stranger was prohibited

or severely restricted. In this connexion, the city
State of Carthage provides an early example of that
egotistic colonial regime which was to form a conspicuous part of the Mercantile System of some
modern nation States.[4] Further, the history not
only of Carthage but largely also that of the power
which overcame her is, we have been told, to be
explained on mercantile lines. The Roman world-
conquest has been represented as the result of a
nationalist concentration on commercial supremacy.[5]
We have been asked to regard Rome as possessing, in
her period of empire-building, a civilization not
materially different from that of modern Europe,
particularly in the seventeenth and eighteenth
centuries, and to note in her foreign policy the influence of conceptions similar to those set forth by
the mercantilist writers of that age. Such episodes
in the Roman advance as the reduction of Greece, the
destruction of Corinth, and the annexation of Carthage
have been stressed as incidents in the career of an
aggressive commercial nationalism. Roman imperialism, in brief, has been pictured as proceeding from
economic considerations resembling in spirit that of
the imperialism of modern European powers.[6]

There is need of much discrimination, however, in
regard to this exceedingly modernist interpretation
of ancient history. That economic causes were
actively at work in the course of events leading to the
Peloponnesian War is obvious, but it is equally plain
that other factors were in operation, and it is not at
all clear that the economic were even the predominant
consideration. And so with some other wars of Greek

history that have been similarly interpreted.[7] The case for Carthaginian Mercantilism, to the extent and within the limits indicated, is less disputable. But it has to be remembered that our impressions concerning Carthage have been derived mainly from hostile accounts which have come down to us, without check from native chronicles, and with little confirmation as yet from archæological discoveries. Such versions of Roman imperialism as are conveyed to us by Mommsen and Ferrero have been forcibly challenged in recent years by Professor Tenney Frank and others, who argue that the passages usually cited give no real support to the theory, which rests not so much upon the testimony of the ancient records as upon ideas read into them from the history of modern times. The republican government apparently took little interest in foreign trade, and Rome certainly did not behave towards her conquests as we should expect her to have done if commercial expansion had been her determining motive. Under the Empire, the wars of Rome were almost invariably defensive in origin or purpose.[8] The economic interpretation of history, which finds congenial subject-matter in the rise and fall of Carthage, has been pressed too far, it would seem, in the attempt to expound the bases of Greek and Roman civilization.

The shortage of the precious metals in the late centuries of antiquity led the Roman State to adopt something in the nature of bullionist expedients at times by restricting the export of these and drawing as much of the currency as possible into its own hands, but its policy was by no means consistent in

this direction, and neither Rome nor any other ancient
State arrived at the conception, which was to be so
closely associated with the Mercantile System and
helped mainly to give it the name, that the best way
in which to procure treasure was to maintain such a
balance of trade as would bring into the country a
larger quantity of money than that which it took out
—or at the connected notion of an import tariff
designed for the protection of native products. It
can hardly be questioned that lack of bullion was one
of the contributory factors in the decline of the Roman
civilization, and it is customary to account for this in
large part on mercantilist principles by referring to a
tremendous drain of gold and silver to the East to pay
for imports that were not offset by exports. But the
evidence on this point is slight and doubtful, and the
actual extent of the export trade has not been
sufficiently regarded.[9] The fact of the shortage is
indeed adequately explicable without resort to the
assumption of an unfavourable balance of commerce.

The Mercantilism of antiquity, such as it was,
tended to be destructive in its ultimate effects. If
Carthage supplies us with a precedent for mercantilist colonial policy, the failure of her dependants
to stand by her in the hour of danger points forward
to the fate of colonial dominions under the modern
mercantilist regime. The excessive State regimentation of industry and commerce which came to prevail
alike in the Hellenistic and the western portions of the
ancient world, and which reached its climax about the
middle of the fourth century of our era,[10] marks that
loss of economic freedom which was a potent cause of

the breakdown of the Græco-Roman civilization.
With the fall of the Empire in the west, involving a
relapse into natural or barter economy—though in
the Byzantine or Eastern Empire a money economy
was retained—the politico-economic evolution of
western Europe had to make a fresh beginning.

CHAPTER III

FACTORS IN THE RISE OF THE MODERN MERCANTILE SYSTEM

RECENT research has brought us to a far better acquaintance with what used to be disparaged as the Dark Ages, and there is a tendency in some quarters to exalt mediaeval civilization as much as it was at one time the fashion to condemn it. But the more we learn about it the more necessary does it seem to hold a course midway between the one and the other extreme. We are concerned in it with a world of theory and a world of actuality, and have continually to take account at once of their mutual influence and of their divergence.[1]

The dissolution of the old order in the west might appear to have given a death-blow to any unitary scheme of civilization. Yet the conception of unity, partly derived from the old Roman imperialism and partly encouraged by the growth of the Catholic faith and Church, retained a strong hold on the minds of men, and it found in time a centre in that anomalous creation, ostensibly a Christianized restoration, the Holy Roman Empire, which brought the notion of the oneness of Christendom, with Emperor and Pope as heads thereof, into the foreground of political and ecclesiastical theory, which it occupied somewhat to the neglect of the developing realities of the age—

the divisions which actually existed and the new forms which in some regions they were tending to assume, though these in turn came gradually to exercise a reactive influence upon theory.   The effective political units were in truth many and varied.   Men governed, or found themselves governed, in communes, feudal lordships, city States, or territorial princedoms, with in some countries the nation State slowly acquiring coherence.   The units of economic organization were those of the household, the manor, the village community, the town, the league of cities.   Anything in the nature of territorial or national economy was only in process of becoming.   The growth of nation States of a kind hardly known to the peoples of antiquity, with a specialized national economy, and the advance of money economy at the expense of the natural economy to which western Europe had returned with the break-up of the old empire, were essential factors in the formation of the Mercantile System.

The unmodified teaching of the Church, which dominated the world of thought and theory, did not favour either of these developments.   It urged the unity of Christendom rather than its division into self-regarding States, and human brotherhood rather than exclusive nationalism.   It looked upon the advance of money economy as involving in practice the pursuit of gain without labour, and condemned usury, or the taking of interest, both on Christian principles and on the Aristotelian ground that it was unnatural.[3]   But the force of circumstances operated strongly against the preservation of a rigid attitude towards these movements on the part of ecclesiastical authority. Thus, the Crusades, blest by the Church for their religious purpose, had as one of their main results a great extension of the range of commerce and consequently of the money economy. It has been said that the religious internationalism represented by the Crusades prepared men's thoughts for economic internationalism, and the twelfth and thirteenth centuries are undoubtedly characterized by the appearance of more liberal arrangements for exchange amongst the communities of Europe.[3] But as time went on the ultimate effect was seen in the strengthening and expansion of the ambitions of rulers, aiming at the development of their dominions into unified States, with centralized economies, adequately equipped for rivalry in commerce and otherwise with other politico-economic organizations. So it came about that the canonists, who set forth the rules of the Church in relation to all departments of human conduct, adapted their teaching to the actualities which they saw about them, so as to regulate as far as possible tendencies which could not be suppressed, and in doing so they gradually evolved, by the end of the fifteenth century, a comprehensive and systematic economic doctrine with a real bearing on concrete conditions.[4] The influence of Church teaching was partly direct and partly indirect, partly intended and partly unintended. Its emphasis on the principle of association arising out of the belief in human brotherhood had doubtless stimulated the development of those local units of gild and municipality which in their economic policy pointed the way for the national economies that were to imitate and largely supersede them. The stress which the Church laid upon the need to control industry and commercial operations in the interests of community was translated in the town systems to the interests not of brotherhood but merely of the local group as distinguished from other local groups—a version afterwards carried over into the national sphere. Moreover, the change whereby the canonists gave limited allowance to features of money economy which had previously fallen under their condemnation was in fact a step towards that exaltation of money which was characteristic of the fully developed Mercantile System, whilst writers like Nicholas Oresme,[5] who, though not breathing the mercantilist spirit, treated economic questions from the standpoint of the nation rather than of the individual or the municipality, put themselves in the line of the evolution of those national economies in which Mercantilism was to be worked out.

As already remarked, it was the exclusive town economies that set the example for the exclusive national economy of the Mercantile System.[6] The history of the rise and development of towns and town economies presents many points of difficulty, about which it is impossible to speak with assurance, but it seems clear that Mercantilism, in its essential sense, had its systematic beginnings in the urban organizations. Urban self-consciousness aimed first at freedom from the oppressive or vexatious requirements of lords or over-lords, and then at the acquisition of the privileges of an independent community. In all lands the towns evolved what may be described as a civic Mercantilism. The common scheme was one of restriction and monopoly, whether in the interests of particular trades, or in the interests of consumers within the town, or in the interests of the town as an economic unit as distinct from other towns or the surrounding country. Industry within the precincts was subjected to a multitude of regulations as to price, quality, and marketing, and against the outside world protective barriers were raised. Custom and practice varied in different lands, and within the same country some towns would make mutual concessions, whilst others would combine for the management of their common trading interests ; but, though there was much more inter-urban freedom in practice than in theory, the economy of the town was in general one of municipal egoism, aiming at the protection of home industry and the maintenance of a favourable balance in its dealings with other districts. Tolls and customs were placed on the entrance of goods into its borders, and the settlement of strangers within the liberties was viewed with suspicion or hostility except where there was some obvious benefit to be derived from it by the urban community. In Germany, where the central authority was weak, the free cities acquired great wealth and power, and followed a purely self-regarding course which made them a serious stumbling-block in the way of the establishment of a German unity which should be more of a reality than that which nominally existed, though the mercantile federation of the Hanse cities pointed in the direction of a national commercial regime. But perhaps Italy affords, in the oligarchic Venetian republic, the most conspicuous example of the mediaeval city as a thoroughly organized economic unit, pursuing an exclusive mercantile policy. Venice, indeed, sought to maintain herself as a separate nation. Her widespread commerce was subjected to the most detailed State regulation. The government dictated the routes to be taken by the merchant fleets, which were convoyed by war vessels, the duration of voyages, the cargoes to be carried, and the prices at which merchandise should be brought and sold. Moreover, the government itself engaged in commercial ventures and retained a monopoly in some commodities. Home industries were developed along with commerce and the carrying trade, and were protected by a tariff which was practically prohibitive. Some justification may be pleaded for this rigid regimentation in view of the dangers to commerce from piracy and war which had led to its establishment, but it is certain that the system was kept up after it had ceased to serve its purpose. The embargo on competition helped to induce indolence amongst the people and the loss of those qualities which had created the power it was designed to uphold, and the manner in which Venice attempted to exploit the territory which she acquired in her own interest alone was a contributory factor in her decline.[7]

The formation of the nation States of modern Europe is a process which has lasted for many centuries right down to our own times. England was early in the attainment of a national unity. The attachment of the French territories directly to the Crown and the bringing of the several parts of Spain under the sway of one royal house were not completed till the sixteenth century, when also various national States of secondary rank which had been developing their identities during the later Middle Ages were in more or less assured existence. Germany, despite her formal unity under an elective king, was really much divided. The territorial princedom was there the predominant political form. In Italy the city State flourished. The national evolution of both Germany and Italy was hindered by their association with the Holy Roman Empire, and they had to wait till the nineteenth century for their triumphs of unity. The work of unification and consolidation in earlier times involved the assertion of the power of the central government over both feudal and municipal elements of local independence, and the growth of the territorial or national State was accompanied by the development of a policy whereby the ruler sought to extend his control to all departments of activity within the range of his dominions. With the expansion of commerce and the opening out of economic interests generally the association of economic with political unity was a natural tendency in the minds of princes and their ministers, and it is hardly surprising that as their policy becomes more coherent they should be found endeavouring to carry out on the larger scale of the territorial or national State a policy similar in spirit to the self-regarding, exclusive, protective economies of the towns, town leagues, and city States of the Middle Ages.

The rise of the New Monarchy, as it is called, in

western Europe, with its ideal of a consolidated dynastic or national power, is one aspect of the movement known as the Renaissance. The revival of learning helped ultimately to promote the emergence of the individual in society, but the humanists were disposed to look largely to the princely or royal power for assistance in the work of freeing the spirit of man from its mediaeval bonds, and thus to emphasize the competence of the State in the ordering of the life of the community. Hence, in its transitional significance, their teaching partly reflected and partly influenced the conception of a ruler who should exercise a sort of paternal authority for the benefit of his people, and of a State or national economy framed in the interests of the prosperity, strength, and independence of the political unit under his control. The Renaissance derived much of its spirit from pagan antiquity. The Reformation based itself on a return to Christian antiquity. But in respect of their political significance in its bearing on the matter in hand, there is little distinction to be drawn between them. In each the secular power was exalted. It has been said that the greatest achievement of the Reformation was the modern State.[8] It has also been remarked, with regard to England, that the Reformation was the greatest achievement of the national State.[9] These apparently conflicting utterances simply point to the fact that the Reformation and the modern State alike were products of a movement away from mediaeval conditions and limitations. The order varied in different countries. In some cases the adoption of Protestantism illustrated the power exercised by the State. In others it fell in with a programme for the establishment of a strong national or princely State. But the idea of the power of the State was equally in favour amongst rulers where the old religious system was pursued, and in its economic aspects it found expression in the Mercantilism of both Catholic and Protestant countries.[10]

The exploratory enterprise of the fifteenth and sixteenth centuries brought distant territories in both the eastern and western hemispheres under the control of European powers, and led to the introduction of the exclusive mercantilist spirit into their colonial regimes, on the lines of Carthaginian and Venetian precedent and example. The discovery of America gave Spain not only a colonial empire, but an abundant supply of precious metals at a time when there was much need in Europe of an addition to the quantity available, and whilst it made Spain a bullionist power, the contrasted position of other countries helped to promote in them the development of a theory, that of the balance of trade, which was to be especially associated with the Mercantile System. The later Middle Ages are marked on the one hand by a growth of commerce and spread of money economy, and on the other hand by a dwindling in the supply of the precious metals by which that economy must be supported, and the cities and States of Europe were much concerned to maintain their stock even if they might not hope largely to increase it. The want and lust of gold and the hope to make or find it played their part in causing debasement of coinage, encouraging the vogue of alchemy, and stimulating exploration. It also influenced the nature of the relations that were being evolved between one country or State and another. Both Aristotle and the canonists had condemned exchanges between individuals where, as they held, one man's gain must mean the other man's loss. The view was now extending that the same principle held good in the commerce of nations and other communities, but it was accepted as a fact without condemnation, and it was felt that as money was urgently needed, care must be taken that the gain, which was estimated in terms of money, should be on the right side. The forbidding of the export of the precious metals was a crude expedient for conserving the country's supply. The devices by which it was sought so to control individual transactions with foreigners that no money should leave the country were more complicated, but still did not rest upon any general idea concerning the country's trade as a whole. But the balance-of-trade doctrine was conceived at any rate as early as the latter part of the fourteenth century, and the great influx of precious metals from the west in the sixteenth combined with the expansion of commerce to bring increasingly forward in the policy of States, even where it was not consciously formulated, an idea which connected the procurement of treasure with the proper development and management of foreign trade.

Spain could obtain bullion direct from the mines. But countries with no such resources must obviously get what they wanted by indirect means. The love of money was common to all. It had increased with

the growth of commerce. Moreover, the advance of
territorial and national States was attended by an
intensification of national and princely jealousies,
which resulted in frequent wars, and, according to
the old saying, money was the sinews of war. It
is true that Machiavelli criticized this maxim. Contrary to the vulgar notion, he tells us, not money but
good soldiers are the sinews of war. Money cannot
procure good soldiers, but good soldiers can procure
money.[11] These observations are connected with
his emphasis on the value of national armies, which
fought for something besides money, as against
mercenary troops, which fought for nothing, or little,
else, and his stress on the need of a national army
was in complete harmony with the general spirit of
Mercantilism in its broadest sense, which aimed, in
England, at any rate, not simply at the filling of the
treasury, but at the nourishment of a vigorous population from which good soldiers could be drawn.
But the value currently set upon money both as
commercial capital and as political treasure, led, with
the increase of the supply in Europe—for Spain did
not succeed in keeping her bullion to herself—to the
more careful working out in practice and in theory of
the idea of the favourable balance of trade. Money
circulating within the realm, it was argued, added
nothing to the wealth of the State. This could best
be increased by an economic policy which at once
assisted and controlled foreign trade in such a way
that the country sold more to other countries than
it bought from them. Whatever Spain might do,
it seemed that any other nation could most surely

obtain the wealth it wanted by successfully regulating the balance of its trade.   In this process also the strength and independence of the country would be furthered by the encouragement given to home industries.

CHAPTER IV

HISTORY OF ENGLISH MERCANTILISM
I. THE PRE-COLONIAL PERIOD

T HE history of English Mercantilism is distinguished by the comprehensive illustration it affords of the several phases of the general subject. By reason of her insular position, England was especially prompted to the trial of a self-regarding economic policy, and as the building up of a national system proceeded mercantilist features soon began to appear. The definite establishment of Mercantilism followed upon the result of the Hundred Years War, which had the effect of making England almost absolutely insular in regard to the Continent, and the undoubted prevalence of Mercantilism ensued when that insularity had been made absolute by the loss of Calais. The expansion of England across the seas in the Elizabethan and Stuart periods gave her the opportunity for extending the range of exclusiveness into her colonial policy. Later, the loss of the old American plantations and the lead that England took in the Industrial Revolution brought about conditions which moved her to abandon a system that was obviously outworn and inapplicable to the transformed and new situation.

But though these sequences are fairly clear, the history of the rise, development and fall of the English mercantile system is by no means a simple matter, and there is need for much further research into both mediaeval and modern economy before the subject can be dealt with satisfactorily. There is legitimate difference of opinion as to when we are to find the beginnings of Mercantilism in our national policy—a problem which requires a resolution of the question as to how far measures which are mercantilist in their practical bearing were conceived upon mercantilist principles by those who framed them or were parts of any consistent scheme of policy at all. There is also the recurring doubt as to how far the Mercantilism of the statute book or order in council was enforced in practice and was therefore accountable for some of the benefits or evils which are put down to it, and lately the question has been raised as to whether with regard to agriculture and the corn trade there was not an intermediate stage between the dominance of local economies and that of national economic regulation, which would give the effective Mercantilism of the State in this department a much shorter life than has been usually supposed.[1]

'It seems certain that the towns first fully developed that policy of economic exclusiveness which when it is employed, with adaptations, on the larger basis of the State we label Mercantilism. Schmoller has given a brilliant survey of the reign of municipal egoism in Germany, though he perhaps exaggerated the degree of its actual realization. In England there was clearly more freedom of inter-municipal trade, but the general spirit was much the same.[2] The ruling aim alike of gild and of burgess body was the advantage of the local craft or the local community. The restrictive practices which we associate with mediaeval town economy seem to have been mainly evolved by local custom, and grants by charter were often nothing more than a formal, purchased register of rights and privileges which had been actually enjoyed long before. The main features of the system have already been indicated. In England, as in Germany, the whole commercial and industrial life of the urban community was regulated by authority which rested, here or there, on a narrower or broader basis. In some cases the management of a business or craft was in the hands of the gild or company, but yet under the ultimate, though sometimes little more than nominal, control of the local magistrates. In others the magistrates exercised direct authority, especially in trades or occupations which were concerned with the food and drink of the people, with beer and bread and victuals. Internally, the municipality protected, on the one hand, the several trades as economic units, and, on the other hand, the whole of the townsfolk regarded as consumers. In its external aspect the town stood forth as an economic unit seeking to regulate its transactions or those of its citizens with the outside world to the benefit of the municipal economy. The stranger had to pay toll on bringing goods into the town, or attending its markets—the object being partly revenue and partly the protection of home industry, and in all its relations with other districts, whether with surrounding country from which the town obtained food supplies and to which it sold the products of its industry, or with other boroughs, it was the aim of the municipality to establish a balance of advantage in its favour against the "foreigner." His operations were liable to other restrictions, besides those of toll and team. He could not sell retail within the liberties and was forbidden on pain of forfeit of the goods to sell to another stranger there. His settlement was commonly regarded with suspicion, only allowed when it was not likely to bring any charge upon the town, and only welcomed when it was likely to bring some stimulus to the industry of the community. At the same time, many towns had a free list so far as petty customs are concerned, whilst some had a general chartered freedom in this direction, and urban economy tended generally to be much less rigid in its working than in the letter of its law.

The system sketched above, even where it failed to maintain prosperity for the self-regarding burgesses, and though it was increasingly defied by the spirit of enterprise, continued to form the main basis of municipal policy until well into modern times.[3] The predominance of the national over the local unit was slow in making itself felt, and the culminating period of mediaeval town economy in England came after the beginning of the process whereby the crown was seeking to substitute national for local regulation. Certain it is that, over a long period, national self-consciousness in the economic sphere was much less pronounced than local self-consciousness, and unable to compete successfully with it, and that the policy evolved by the urban units had an important formative influence upon that developed by the national unit.[4]

Something in the nature of a preparatory basis

3

for the establishment of a national economy in England was laid by Edward I, in the work of definition and consolidation to which he addressed himself after the constitutional struggles of his father's reign, and the trend of public policy from that time forward was in the direction of a protective and assertive economic nationalism, but with much inconsistency and incoherence and with many interruptions and reversals owing to political and financial exigencies and the varied characters and aims of successive monarchs and ministers, and with the execution of the law in which the intentions of government were expressed always falling far behind its literal requirements.

The main foundation of England's wealth in the Middle Ages was the " golden fleece," and the beginnings of English Mercantilism are perhaps to be traced in the early measure for the fostering of a native woollen manufacture. At least as far back as the twelfth century there were weavers up and down the country, and, in the next, Simon de Montfort showed himself a pioneer of industrial protection by carrying through the Oxford Parliament orders that English wool should not be sent abroad, but should be worked up at home, and that most of the people should use cloth made in England. These decisions had little effect in the intended directions, but the idea of protection had taken root. Before the end of Henry III's reign, and again under Edward II—who, like Simon, tried to discourage the purchase of foreign cloth—there were proposals to improve the manufacture by inviting artisans from the Continent, and Edward III has been commonly credited with having given the first great stimulus to the home industry by bringing over Flemish workmen to teach their craft to native apprentices, and forbidding both the export of English wool and the import of foreign cloth. It would seem, however, from the most recent investigations of the history of the wool trade, that the influence of the Flemish immigration on the early growth of the manufacture has been somewhat over-emphasized.[5] Moreover, not only did the fluctuating position of the King cause modification of the protective legislation, but even when formally in force it was actually little regarded. Still, it is significant as marking the initiation of what was to be a leading branch of the English Mercantile System —the nourishment and safeguarding of an industry that was England's chief staple till King Cotton displaced King Wool as the result of the Industrial Revolution. The woollen manufacture became the constant care of the State, and regulations were framed again and again for its proper carrying on. The history of the trade, however, provides striking evidence both of the failure of special campaigns of stimulation and of the manner in which statutory and administrative rules—whether good or bad—were evaded or defied. State intervention was often much less well-informed than it was well-meaning, and it had far less to do with the advance of the industry than the co-existence of statutes and orders on the one hand and an increasing manufacture on the other in itself might lead us to infer.[6]

The French wars of Edward III, which were distinguished by the great national victories of Crécy and Poitiers, and inspired the first jingo poet, Laurence Minot, undoubtedly helped to strengthen national self-consciousness, and something of this effect, deferred, it is true, is possibly to be discerned in the appearance, though not the uniform maintenance, under Richard II, of a policy which presents distinct mercantilist features. Thus a law was passed to encourage the export of corn, in the interest of English tillage, and a Navigation Act which, with the declared object of restoring the Navy, sought to restrict both exports and imports to English vessels inaugurated that protection of shipping which was to become a conspicuous part of the mercantilist regime, though this first experiment, like the contemporary corn law, soon broke down in practice. The inadequacy of the supply of bullion, which had been accentuated by the expenditure in the recent wars, led to a veto on exportation. This was simply after the manner of previous prohibitions. But during the discussion of the question there emerged a conception of international trade which was to exercise a powerful influence upon English economic policy.

Richard Aylesbury, officer of the Mint, declared that the lack was due to the spending of too much money on foreign wares, and held that if this matter were properly regulated not only would the money that was in England abide there but plenty more would come from abroad. The aim must be to ensure that foreign merchandise should not be brought into the realm to a value greater than that of the English merchandise which went out.[7] The notion that an injurious drain of money took place through the excessive purchase of commodities from distant lands had found expression in the Roman Empire, but the idea of avoiding a drain of treasure by regulating the balance of trade does not seem to have been enunciated till it was set forth by Richard Aylesbury.

Though the policy that prevailed then and for long afterwards did not rest upon any theory of the balance of trade, it had the same end in view so far as the procurement of a money surplus, or at any rate the avoidance of a money loss, on commercial relations with foreigners, is concerned. The State sought to be present, through the officers of the Staple, at every bargain made in the chief goods exported, and to make such bargain produce bullion. Once bullion was in the country the labour was to prevent it from getting out. Not only was there direct prohibition, but under the Statutes of Employments foreign merchants coming to England were required to spend the money they got for their goods on English manufactures, and by various devices the exchanges were manipulated with the same object of keeping money within the realm.[8]

Mercantilist feeling in the fifteenth century is strikingly illustrated in two popular verse pamphlets on English policy,[9] which were apparently prompted by a feeling of protest against the relaxation of protective governance in the unquiet times of Henry VI, and which have so much in common that they may be treated as one. They breathe a spirit which is not only protectionist but strongly aggressive. The commercial relations of England and other countries are distinguished therein according to their profitable or unprofitable character, and Englishmen are advised not to sell their wares too cheaply. England is urged to exploit her natural and acquired facilities and possibilities—the wool of her sheep, her cloth manufacture, her ability to command the Straits of Dover—in such a manner as to establish over other nations an economic hold which should form the basis of a political supremacy in western Europe.

The course of events at that time was far from furnishing any such development, but it had its effect in helping to stimulate a mercantilist trend in public policy when conditions became more settled. The loss of the French possessions threw England back upon herself, and the subsequent civil war created a situation which seemed to render necessary a strong central government to give the country peace and order and defend it against any attack. Edward IV is sometimes accounted the founder of the New Monarchy in England, and his reign in its economic aspects is characterized not only by bullionist legislation of the usual kind, but by a more comprehensive attempt than had been witnessed before to prevent money from going to the foreigner and to promote native industry by excluding foreign goods. But it was Henry VII who, after bringing the Wars of the Roses to an end, definitely established a strong national dynasty in England. His economic expedients present nothing new, but they were employed for the regulation, protection, and promotion of industry and commerce with a more definite relation to the establishment and maintenance of national prosperity and power than had previously been conceived. They aimed at protecting the home manufacturer from foreign competition, whilst favouring the importation of such raw materials as he might require, and a notable series of commercial treaties was made with the object of recovering old and securing new markets. There was also the usual veto on the exportation of bullion. To the end of restoring the mercantile marine, bounties were offered for the construction of large ships, and Navigation Acts were passed to limit the importation of French wares to English vessels manned by English sailors. Henry's attempts at economic control were to a large extent ineffective, but the peace and order which he gave to England were conducive to industrial and commercial progress and the increase of national wealth, though much of the treasure that the King himself heaped up was gained by methods doubtful in themselves and of only temporary practicability.

Under Henry VIII the royal power was exalted to an almost unprecedented pitch, and as the real founder of the modern Navy the second Tudor assisted in the development of an essential element in the English Mercantile System; but important and even revolutionary as his reign is from the economic standpoint, it shows no definite advance in the conception of mercantilist policy.

The reigns of Edward and Mary, with their quick changes and reverses, form a break in the characteristic Tudor period; but it was in the midst of the disturbed conditions of Edward's reign that we get the first statement at any length of some of the main points in the English mercantilist view of national

policy.   This is in the famous dialogue now attributed
to John Hales,[10] particularly in the speeches assigned
to the doctor, which are of especial interest if, as has
been suggested, they represent the views of Latimer.
Industry and agriculture, we read, should be governed
in such a way as to replenish the realm with people
able to defend it and win treasure for the same.
The producers of corn ought to be encouraged by
allowing them free export. This might cause an
immediate rise of prices, but it would be to the benefit
of the realm as a whole in the maintenance of tillage,
and in the end the position as to prices would rectify
itself.   Then come some admirable remarks on the
interdependence of the nations. " It is ordained
that no nation shall have all commodities, so that one
may know they have need of another's help, and
thereby love and society shall grow all the more."
It is impossible to live of ourselves. We cannot live
without the commodities of others. Yet the doctor
is under the influence of the idea that if we buy more
of strangers than we sell to them we impoverish
ourselves and enrich them.   There are, he says,
many things which we obtain from abroad, thus
casting treasure out of the realm, when we ought
either to do without them or to make them ourselves,
thus saving treasure ; and he protests especially
against the sending abroad of raw material which is
there made up into articles that we buy, so that we
pay the stranger for what should be done to the gain
of ourselves.   He divides artificers into three classes—
some, like mercers and vintners, through whom money
is taken out of the country, as they sell wares growing

beyond the seas ; others, like shoemakers and tailors and brewers, who get and spend all within the country but bring in no treasure ; and others, like clothiers, who bring in treasure by their sales abroad. The first could best be spared. The last we must cherish. If we but fostered these and men of other trades, they could make us not only enough for ourselves, but a surplus to send over the sea and so bring us necessary commodities and treasure.

It was in the reign of Elizabeth that Mercantilism of the more moderate and more liberal kind first found regular and consistent expression in England. The policy of Burleigh has indeed been eulogized as " the high-water mark " of English Mercantilism, which is seen at its best, we have been told, in the measures that he adopted for procuring and sustaining the prosperity and power of England.[11] They followed generally on the lines recommended by Hales, but differed in certain respects both from earlier tentatives and from later developments. Thus Cecil was greatly concerned for the maintenance of the Navy in the interests of national defence, and took various steps for the promotion of shipping and the nourishment of seamen, especially through bounties on shipbuilding and encouragement of the fisheries ; but he had little sympathy with the restrictive policy of the Navigation Acts. That policy had only been pursued by fits and starts, but it had been resented by foreign powers as being directed to their hurt, with the result that international relations had been disturbed and English merchants had had to suffer. Instead of prohibitions, differential duties were now imposed. Cecil's attitude in this matter was not based on specially liberal principles. Yet it is a fact that the maritime enterprise which is one of the striking features of Elizabeth's reign was little assisted by restrictive legislation against the foreigner. Moreover, Cecil did not lay so much stress upon mere bullion as did some of the Mercantilists. An attempt was indeed made to prevent its export, but with untoward consequences, and in general Cecil sought to replenish the treasury by means of the balance of trade. The one thing which robbed England, he held, was when more merchandise was brought into the realm than was carried out, as the balance must be paid with money. He therefore laboured to bring about a reduction in the use of such foreign commodities as were not essential, and aimed at encouraging home industries, both to meet home requirements and to produce for export. Patents were granted to individuals or companies for the starting of new industries, for the better organization of existing industries, or the development of trade in specified regimes, such as Spain, Russia, the Baltic, the Levant, and, after Burleigh's death, the East Indies. Especial attention was paid to those forms of production and those occupations which seemed necessary for the maintenance of a vigorous population, and for the requirements of defence in time of war. This aim is to be traced in what was done or attempted for the encouragement or even enforcement of tillage, the fostering of the fisheries and shipping, the development of mineral resources, the establishment of the manufacture of ordnance, and the control of that of gunpowder. An endeavour was also made to regulate industry in the interests of the State and commonwealth by introducing a national and compulsory system of trade apprenticeship and making labour in craft, or service, or agriculture compulsory ; and the problem of poverty was dealt with by the gradual building up of a general poor law.

There can be no doubt that many of the things aimed at by the Elizabethan government were to a large extent attained. It has indeed been claimed that its measures were brilliantly successful, and that much of the progress of the century was due to the deliberate efforts and interference of Cecil. But the more we examine the evidence, the more doubtful we become as to the degree to which the government policy was actually operative, and how far the national advance was due to it. The most careful students of the patent system contend that it was on the whole more hurtful than helpful in its effects.[12] The granting of monopolies, especially in the latter part of the reign, was certainly carried to excess. In many cases they involved practically a tax on industry and the consumer for the benefit of persons who rendered no countervailing public service. Moreover, the constitution and proceedings of some of the companies for foreign trade were criticized, not without reason, as favouring London to the disadvantage of other parts of the country, as tending to keep up prices, and as causing resentment against England in the lands where they traded.[13] The attempt to set up a uniform apprenticeship system was on the whole a failure. The government had

not the requisite machinery to enforce it, and in
practice the more flexible and variable system evolved
by the trade gilds and companies prevailed.[14] In
this and in other connexions the industrious efforts
of the Privy Council to make real the national control
which it was sought to establish were by no means so
effective as has been commonly inferred. Tudor
attempts to regulate England's chief staple industry,
that of wool, were almost as fruitless as those of other
reigns, and recent research has shown that the intentions of Crown and Parliament had little effect in
initiating or influencing economic development in
the corn trade—a remark which applies also to the
contemporary royal tentatives in France. The official
policy was on the whole to consider the producer, and
the aim was to discourage importation and to encourage corn production alike for home requirements and
so as to obtain a surplus for export which might bring
treasure or useful commodities into the realm. But,
so far as this was the clearly conceived national policy,
it was found impossible to carry it out with consistency.
In times of scarcity, the needs of the consumer were of
necessity the prime consideration. Export was forbidden, but the position was often rendered worse
by the restrictions which it was thought necessary to
place on the operations of the middlemen. In normal
times the statutory policy was rendered nugatory
by the administrative action which was forced upon
the Council by the dominance of London as a consumer
of corn. The rapid growth of London at the expense
of rural districts and of other towns caused her during
the sixteenth century to draw to herself the corn

supplies of perhaps the larger part of the country, and to determine the prices for that area. Her demand indeed tended to outrun the organized supply, and even to involve requirements from abroad. Hence it came about that it was the position of London in regard to the satisfaction of her own needs that controlled the action of the government in allowing or restricting importation on the one hand or exportation on the other, so that its policy was rather metropolitan than national, often to the disadvantage of important corn-producing regions.[15] In relation to bullion, though the normal Elizabethan policy contrasts favourably with that of Spain, who, as owner of the western mines, attached an exaggerated significance to it, the government yet did not reject the gain of treasure brought in by privateering expeditions. The prosperity thus produced was, however, more apparent than real.   It led to reprisals by Spain, which caused a depression of trade, and this helped to make the financing of the struggle against the Armada very difficult.[16]

The Elizabethan age was one of economic progress, despite the " other side " of poverty ; but such considerations as have been presented above prevent us from assigning too large a share to a system of national control in the mixture of State policy, local economy, and private initiative and enterprise by which the results of the reign were achieved.

CHAPTER V

HISTORY OF ENGLISH MERCANTILISM
II. THE COLONIAL PERIOD

UNDER Elizabeth the expansion of England upon and across the seas had begun. With the Stuarts comes the great epoch of English colonization. Ireland and Scotland are brought into new relations with England. Parliament has become more assertive, while the Crown has a stubborn notion of the divine right of kings, and we get two revolutions and an interregnum. In the following century, after a struggle with France which brings imperial gain, we have a colonial revolution which leads to imperial loss. With all these circumstances and events the development and fortunes of the mercantilist theory and system are bound up, and it is to this age that the literature of Mercantilism mainly belongs. It is impossible, even if it were desirable, to enter here into the minutiæ and technicalities of the factors which affected the elaboration of the mercantilist theory or the variations in its practical application. We can only look at some of the main aspects of what may be called the colonial period in English mercantilist history.

It is perhaps not to be wondered at that an exaggerated notion of the need of treasure should'prevail amongst those who studied or were responsible for public policy in the late sixteenth and early seventeenth century, when the Crown, largely from general causes beyond its own control, was constantly in a state of financial embarrassment. The influx of precious metals from the New World had caused a rise in prices in the Old. The expenses of government had increased and were increasing, but the royal revenue had not been placed on such a basis as would be adequate to meet the changed conditions. By conciliating Parliament James I and Charles I might have made some progress towards the desired end ; but whilst Parliament was becoming more assertive owing to the growing strength of the middle class and the freedom from external danger, the Crown held to theories of government which brought it repeatedly into conflict with the Commons, and questions of public economy were fought out both in Parliament itself and between King and Parliament.

Both James and Charles aimed, as Cecil had done, at controlling the economic life of the subjects of the Crown in the interests of political and national power. Their ablest advisers, particularly Bacon and Wentworth, belonged to the mercantilist school in their views on the balance of trade and State regimentation, and there is a family resemblance between the expedients of the first two Stuarts and those which Burleigh had adopted, in the way of industrial and commercial regulation. But the care of James I and Charles for the economic welfare of the country as they conceived it was interrupted and often counteracted by the exigencies of their constitutional relations. In not a few cases, moreover, it was as ill-judged as it was well-meaning, and its exercise was frequently thwarted, as it was frequently dictated, from below. A strong feeling for self-direction still prevailed amongst many of the towns, and there were growing industrial areas which had not known a restrictive urban economy and that looked with suspicion on State control, so that local spirit often fought against the resolutions of central authority, whilst in the spheres of foreign trade, adventurous interlopers challenged the ground of the chartered companies. Certainly, under the first two Stuarts the economic progress of England cannot be said either to have been much indebted to power in the political administration or to have contributed much to it, and its fruits helped to give Parliament the victory which meant revolution.

The early years of James are marked by an interesting controversy between the advocates of " free " and of regulated trade. The views of the " free traders " had not the scope that we nowadays associate with the name. They were not concerned with the removal of barriers against the foreigner, but were simply protesting against the concession to companies of merchants—whether joint stock, or of independent traders operating under a common rule and government—of the sole right of trade in specific foreign parts. Yet to the extent of their protest they set forth some of the principles upon which the argument for general freedom of trade has been founded.[1] "All free subjects," they say, " are born inheritable as to their land, so also to the free exercise of their industry in those trades whereto they apply themselves and whereby they are to live. Merchandise being the chief and richest of all other, and of greater extent and importance than all the rest, it is against the natural right and liberty of the subjects of England to restrain it into the hands of some few, as now it is." They advocated the removal of all restrictions in the interests of enlargement of trade, a wider distribution of its benefits, an increase of shipping and mariners and of " the wealth of the general of all the land." Holland was pointed to as a notable illustration of the advantages of freedom—in the sense conceived by the protesters—which enabled the Dutch to win markets at England's expense. The " free traders " were unable to secure a general Act to the effect of their desires, and though they obtained one which declared the trade with France and Spain open, this was soon stultified by the grant of a patent which put the French traffic into the hands of a regulated company. It is difficult to generalize as to what would probably have been the effect of a victory for " free trade " at this time, but the subsequent history of some of the companies would suggest that in these cases the continued possession of monopoly or semi-monopoly was not favourable to enterprise, and that in the spheres which they cultivated the persistence of regulation contributed to the advance, real and comparative, of the Dutch commerce, which was regarded with peculiar jealousy as well as admiration by the country which had helped the Dutch in their struggle for independence.

Without dwelling upon the obvious abuses of the prerogative, we may say that James I was particularly unfortunate in his endeavour to influence by royal

4

interference the course of English industry and commerce in the interests of national wealth and power. Thus he took into his own hands the manufacture of alum, important for its use in cloth-making, with unsatisfactory results, and his deliberate attempt at once to force and to foster home industry and foreign trade in finished cloth was not only unsuccessful but positively harmful in its effects.

The Netherlands had at one time provided a market for English wool, and with the development of the English manufacture an export trade to that country in white and unfinished cloths had been established, but finished English cloths were not welcomed there. The English government, however, viewed with disapproval a trade which, though profitable in itself, gave employment to the foreigner, which meant, as it seemed, a loss to English finishers. Hence both under the Tudors and under James attempts were made to check or to remedy the supposed grievance by either forbidding the trade altogether or insisting upon the inclusion of one finished for every ten unfinished cloths in all outward shipments. In practice, however, exemptions were granted pretty freely, and a good deal of English white cloth was exported by the Merchant Adventurers by licence, to be finished in Holland. With the improvement in English methods, however, a growing trade in finished cloths was developed in further regions, and apparently it was sought to press the trade in the Flemish market. This attempt led to a direct prohibition from the Flemish side of the import of any but white cloths from England. The cloth-workers and dyers of London resented the veto, and with the object of fostering in England the trade of dyeing, dressing, and finishing, and forcing the Flemish market, James was induced to listen to a project involving the absolute requirement that every cloth sent from England should be dyed and finished before leaving the country. The Merchant Adventurers, who from their knowledge of the foreign market had always been opposed to the restriction, refused to lend the King any assistance. A proclamation, however, was issued, forbidding the exportation of unfinished cloths, except to a specified extent, which was to be allowed pending the settlement of the trade. Then James, maintaining his " princely resolution " against impediments and difficulties, chartered a Company of King's Merchants of the New Trade who were to take the English dyed cloths to the foreign market.

The scheme, however, was an utter failure. The Dutch closed their ports to English cloths of all kinds and a tariff war with Holland and other countries followed, with bad effects long after the scheme itself had been abandoned. The new company, unable to find a market, were not in a position to buy up the cloths finished in England. In the serious disorganization of both the export and the domestic trade which obtained, both weavers and finishers and the promoters of the design suffered. Proposals were made, on the one hand, to punish the Venturers who refused to take the cloth and, on the other, to find a vent for it in the immediate future by compelling the use of broadcloth by councillors, courtiers, and their servants, but these came to nothing. The project was abandoned, the company was dissolved, and the old Merchant Venturers were restored, but it was some years before the trade recovered from the confusion. In a proclamation on the subject it was confessed that there would have been more loss in the making of cloth than gain in the dyeing and dressing of it. "Time," admitted the Solomon of England, "discovereth many disabilities that cannot at first be seen."[2]

The German economist List, who was full of admiration for the policy of England, as he interpreted it, in its mercantilist phases, commends the shrewdness of Edward III for the plan by which he established the cloth manufacture in England by the aid of foreigners, and then protected it by forbidding imports from abroad. He further notes how an export trade in rough cloth was converted into one wholly of dyed and finely dressed cloths by the measures of protection and encouragement of the art of dressing cloth introduced under James and Charles.[3] Of what Edward III actually did we have already spoken. It is true that James I sought to complete the work which the Plantagenet king was supposed to have begun. It was his desire and resolution that " as the reducing of wools into clothing was the act of our noble progenitor King Edward the Third, so the reducing of the trade of white cloths, which is but an imperfect thing towards the wealth of this our Kingdom, into the trade of cloths died and dressed might be the work of our time." But the collapse of his scheme was patent, and the desired result was to come about by a more natural development of the industry.

Charles I's economic ideas and policy in the main resembled those of his father, and just as the fiasco of the " New Trade " illustrated the risk attending injudicious attempts to force the success of an industry, so the experience of Charles in connexion with the " business and occupation " of soap-making showed the disturbance that might be caused by unwise methods of industrial supervision. Charles paid much attention to commerce, but such economic prosperity as was witnessed during his effective reign was assisted rather by the peace which he was compelled to maintain owing to his lack of money and his quarrels with Parliament than to any definite royal measures of control and regulation.

Charles, like his father, has been represented as exhibiting, in his dealings with the American colonies that were founded during this epoch, little trace of that strong Anglo-centric conception of national interests and power which was later to express itself in measures deliberately aimed at subordinating the interests of the colonies to those of the mother country. But in point of fact, though it is doubtful whether he had formed any clear plan for a self-sufficient empire, he was undoubtedly the real beginner of what is known as the old colonial system, which attained to its full development under his son. Indeed, nearly all its essential features are to be found in tentative existence before the end of Charles I's personal rule. .

Moreover, a mercantilist policy of this type was

consistently applied by Wentworth in Ireland. Wentworth sought to make that country a source of strength to the Crown, of fiscal and military power, and the whole of his industrial and commercial measures there were directed to that end. They were mercantilist for England in regard to Ireland, and for Ireland in respect of other countries, but the paramount claims of England determined all. There was only a very partial recognition of the essential mutuality of advantage in the maintenance of free relations between one country or power and another. Thus the staple trade of England was in cloth. There was a nascent woollen cloth-making industry in Ireland. It was Wentworth's object to crush this manufacture on purely political grounds. It would trench upon the "clothings" of England. Wool "grew" in Ireland in very great quantities, and if the people were allowed to manufacture it, not only would the English lose the profits which they now made by manufacturing Irish wools, but the King would lose in customs, and the English might be driven out of the trade itself by underselling. Besides, in "reasons of State"—here we have a Machiavellian argument applied in the economic sphere—so long as they did not manufacture their own wools, they must of necessity fetch their clothing from England, and so in a way depend upon England for a livelihood, and thereby "become so dependent upon this crown as they could not depart from us without nakedness to themselves and children." Salt was to be a monopoly of the King so as to make the Irish dependent upon him for a necessity in all their native staple commodities. On the other hand, the linen trade was to be revived and encouraged on the ground that it would be beneficial to England and Ireland alike, and all at the expense of the foreigner. Indeed, the help of foreigners was used for the purpose of cutting the ground from their feet in this matter. Wentworth procured flax seed from Holland, because it was better than the home sort, sent for workmen from the Low Countries and France and with their help established a trade by means of which, as he hoped, the Irish linen cloths would undersell those of Holland and France by at least twenty per cent. In general he endeavoured to develop a " rightly conditioned " commerce, in which the native commodities exported should be greater in value than the foreign commodities imported— " a certain sign that the Commonwealth gathers upon their neighbours."[4] The material prosperity of the country was much advanced under Wentworth's rule, but his work was largely destroyed by the rebellion which followed the removal of his strong hand, and during the subsequent Civil War, and his policy set an evil precedent. We can well understand the apprehensions that might be entertained concerning an Irish competition in the cloth trade, but the temporary disorganization that this might have caused in the English industry could have been only a small matter as compared with the ill-effects, in after times, of the regime, inaugurated by Wentworth, in which the economic interests of Ireland were subordinated to the supposed interests of England.

The Stuart system of economic control was broken up by the Civil War, and internal strife inevitably caused a serious interruption of trade. Cromwell has often been depicted as a brilliant mercantilist statesman and ruler, who at this juncture promoted a revival of commerce and extended the bounds of the empire by a policy which bears the clear impress of the orthodox economic beliefs of the time.[5] " Cromwell's Navigation Act " has been cited again and again as the palmary example of the way in which the State came successfully to the aid of shipping and commerce and as the beginning of a regime, under which, and largely by reason of which, England's naval ascendancy was established. It is perhaps the most famous of all mercantilist measures, and its admirers have been wont to give it a place as a landmark in the development of England's sea-power and commerce in some sort comparable with that assigned to Magna Charta in the history of her constitutional liberties.[6] Moreover, the West Indian expedition of the Protectorate has been viewed as part of a vast scheme for the conquest of the whole of the Spanish possessions in the west, and the acquisition of their mines of precious metals, so that England might become a great bullionist as well as commercial power ; and though its immediate result was simply the capture of Jamaica, it has been regarded as laying the foundation of England's future position as head of a great mercantile colonial empire.[7]

But this estimate of Cromwell's work requires much modification and correction, both as to the facts and as to the effects of his policy. He was by no means a typical mercantilist. Under him the Stuart methods of industrial and commercial regu-

lation were to a large extent abandoned, though in
the later days of his protectorate some of the privileged
companies which had been set aside were restored to
status. It was perhaps rather the exigencies of
circumstance than anti-mercantilist or mercantilist
ideas that determined his attitude and proceedings
in these regards. Cromwell certainly displayed his
concern for trade in the several commercial treaties
which he arranged, but—with the exception of the
Portuguese treaty, of which more anon—these can
hardly be ranked as distinctively mercantilist expedients, and the view that has been widely held
as to "Cromwell's Navigation Act," like the
popular conception of Magna Charta, has been effectively challenged by those who have studied the evidence
most carefully.[8] The first English Navigation Act
as we have seen, belongs to the reign of Richard II.
The exclusive shipping policy of the colonial period
was started not under the Commonwealth but by
Charles I, and there is nothing to suggest that Cromwell
had any share in the Commonwealth Ordinance which
has gone by his name, but which, it would seem, was
really the work of some few interested persons.
Cromwell apparently had no enthusiasm for the
Ordinance, or for the war with the Protestant Dutch
of which it was a provoking cause, though he was not
free from the common jealousy of Dutch commercial
supremacy. So far from benefiting trade, the Ordinance checked a slight revival that was beginning to
make itself felt and produced a further dislocation,
and the assumption that there was a substantial
expansion of commerce under the Protectorate seems

to rest mainly upon customs figures, which were swollen not so much by an increase of traffic, as by a more rigorous exaction and collection of dues.[9] Neither the Ordinance nor its statutory successors, which we shall consider later, caused a decline in Dutch shipping, and there is no definite evidence that they contributed to the increase of English shipping. The obvious mixture of religious, commercial, and merely opportunist motives in Cromwell's counsels makes it difficult to find in the circumstances of the West Indian adventure adequate grounds for the view of him as an ambitious mercantilist imperialist,[10] and whatever may have been the ultimate significance of that expedition, the effect of the breach and war with Spain was further damage to English trade.[11] The enlarged commerce with France which arose out of the Cromwellian alliance was held by mercantilists to be no compensation, because in it the import values greatly exceeded the export. In short, Cromwell's economic policy was neither so mercantilist nor so successful as has been imagined ; but those transactions which have usually been chosen as the most striking illustrations of his Mercantilism contributed seriously to the financial embarrassments of his regime.

All the main features of English mercantilist policy had made their appearance before the Restoration, and with the accession of Charles II the movement took on an expanded life, both in its colonial reference and in that aspect of it to which the name Mercantile System was to be specifically applied—the attempt so to regulate trade with other countries as to secure and preserve a favourable balance for the homeland.

Early in the reign was published Thomas Mun's *England's Treasure by Foreign Trade*, a posthumous work which had been composed about forty years previously.[12]   Mun has been described as the " founder of the Mercantile System."   His treatise, we are told, was received as the gospel of finance and commercial policy, and its title, according to Adam Smith, became a fundamental maxim in the political economy not of England only but of all other commercial countries.[13]   But, as we have seen, the beginnings of English Mercantilism, both in the broad sense in which we are considering it, and in the narrower one of its association with the balance idea, date much farther back than the time when Mun was writing his pamphlets—the balance doctrine was adumbrated before the end of the fourteenth century.   Moreover, throughout the seventeenth century and down to the middle of the eighteenth there was a flow of "discourses on trade " and the like, from Gerard de Malynes to James Steuart,[14] and a development of mercantilist policy under Stuart and Whig regimes, in relation to which it may be said that the teachings of Mun are in some respects an advance upon the general run of mercantilist theory and practice rather than a typical exposition of it.   In none of the writers do we get a systematic setting forth of the aim and mode of national economy of which Mercantilism in the " balance of trade " sense is only a part.   The basis and range of that policy, directed ideally towards prosperity in peace and self-sufficiency and strength in war, .have to be extracted and inferred from the records of theory and practice alike.   The general lines upon which it proceeded have already been indicated, but it may be convenient at this point to summarize them in regard to their main directions.[15] If we were in want of a text none better could be found than that which is supplied by the refrain of a once popular song—

> We don't want to fight, but, by Jingo! if we do,
> We've got the ships, we've got the men, and we've got
>   the money too,

for all the prime elements of English mercantilist policy can be related, directly or indirectly, to the procurement of resources in one or other member of that trinity of contributions to national self-sufficiency and power.

The need of ships was especially dictated to the English nation by geographical considerations, which indeed had a good deal to do with the form taken by English Mercantilism in other connexions. Ships were required alike for the commerce that was to procure wealth and for purposes of defence and offence in war, and the protection and encouragement of shipping was sought even where some other interest, which otherwise it might be desirable to foster, had to be suppressed or restricted in consequence, as when the customs duties which might have accrued from the resort of foreign ships to English ports were sacrificed on behalf of English naval power, or when limitations were placed on the use of timber for other industries— such as the Sussex iron—when it was needed for the building of ships. It was the object of the Navigation Acts to further English shipping by insisting that the traffic between England and the Colonies and other countries should be conducted only in English—or colonial—vessels manned mainly by English—or colonial—seamen ; and in order directly to stimulate the building of big ships bounties were allowed on their construction. Special attention was paid to the fisheries as the school of seamanship—the compulsory observance of fish days had originated in a desire to increase the market—and the encouragement of the production of corn and of manufactures for export was also partly designed to give larger employment to ships and mariners.

The production and nourishment of a vigorous population was another object of Mercantilism, not only as an end desirable in itself but as necessary for national defence and offence. The protection and encouragement of industry generally had partly this purpose, but the policy adopted in regard to tillage and the corn trade was more specifically concerned with it. The various forms of agricultural protection, of which the corn laws and bounties are the most conspicuous examples, originated mainly in regard for the maintenance of an adequate food supply, especially in time of war, and also in the desire to preserve a race of sturdy yeomen and peasants who would make good fighting men. Mercantilists of the more restricted school were interested primarily in the promotion of foreign trade and the protection and encouragement of home manufactures both for domestic requirements and for export. But Mun pointed out the unwisdom of undue concentration on a few staple industries, particularly that of cloth-making. It was certainly " the greatest wealth and best employment " for the poor, but it would be advantageous to practise tillage and fishing more rather than trust so wholly to industry. For in times of war, or on some other occasion, if a foreign prince should prohibit the use of English cloth in his dominions, poverty and disturbance might easily be caused amongst the poor of the country through the loss of their ordinary maintenance. Hence the advantage of a diversity of employments, and the increase of tillage and fishing would mean an increase of plenty, safety, and profit. Thereby many thousands would be able to do the Kingdom good service in time of war, especially by sea. What has already been said as to the encouragement of the fisherman and the mariner has its obvious bearing in this connexion.

But it is the part played by consideration of bullion or treasure in mercantilist theory and practice that has attracted most attention. The development of money economy owing to expanding industrial and commercial relations, the comparative absence of credit, and the growing actual shortage of bullion in the later Middle Ages, and the influx of precious metals from the west, its effect upon prices, and the enlarging needs of national revenue both in peace and in war in the earlier modern age—all these factors tended to induce a specialized attention to money or bullion as a main, if not the main, element in national wealth. The less enlightened idea, arising out of mediaeval conditions and not unnatural to the age, but pursued well into modern times, was that every possible step should be taken to retain in the country the money or bullion already there, and to prevent money that might be brought in from leaving it.   The expedients of prohibition, manipulation of the exchanges, balance of bargains, and Statute of Employments have already been noticed.   With the changing conditions of commerce, such as the disappearance of the Staple system, and the rise and growth of the Merchant Adventurers and other companies for foreign trade, these methods of control became less and less possible and effective, and the balance-of-trade theory, after a period during which it divided opinion with the bullionist and balance-of-bargain ideas, asserted predominance. It was, at any rate, an advance upon those theories, just as a national economy was an advance upon self-regarding local economies.   The doctrine was that in international commerce a country should seek to secure that its exports should exceed its imports, as the balance must then be inevitably paid in treasure or in money.   This, declared Mun, was the only way in which treasure could be obtained, and he held that the old restrictive devices were altogether ineffective.[16] The ordinary means to increase our treasure is by foreign trade, " wherein we must ever observe this rule, to sell more to strangers yearly than we consume of theirs in value "—a rule recommended by Aylesbury and Hales long ago.   The common mercantilist inference was that where trade with a given country involved greater import than export values, it was a " losing " trade and to be discouraged.   Where it meant greater export than import values, it was a " gaining " trade and to be encouraged.   Surveys of the commerce of England with other nations were set forth to show what were " gaining " and what were

" losing " branches. The expedients for promoting a favourable balance of trade included prohibitions, or discriminating tariffs, which should operate against the introduction of foreign manufactured goods, in favour of the import of raw material required from abroad for English manufactures, and also, to a less extent, in favour of goods imported for re-exportation rather than for use. The State also intervened by granting patents for necessary industries, and charters to companies for the promotion of advantageous foreign trades, and applying in various ways its powers of regulation, control, restriction, protection, and promotion to the end of maintaining industrial self-sufficiency and power, and of the increase of treasure and capital at the expense of the foreigner. As time went on, the mercantilist emphasis was laid less on the monetary and more on the industrial aspect of the policy.

The shifting of emphasis from the advantage of retaining or gaining a surplus of the precious metals to the importance of promoting national industry becomes clear about the end of the seventeenth century, and it has been customary to see in this the beginning of Protectionism as distinguished from the older Mercantilism—a development induced by altered conditions as to capital and credit, industry and commerce. The employment of labour was viewed increasingly as an aim of policy, and the state of commerce and the balance were examined with more specific reference to their bearing upon domestic production—the demand for home labour that they created or involved.[17] About the middle of the eighteenth century we find Josiah Tucker giving a new name for the desirable object. What is required, he tells us, is " the balance of industry," for money without industry, he adds, is "a hurt not a blessing." [18] The novelty of this phase is, however, only comparative. As we have seen, the industrial principle had always been present in English Mercantilism, even when the money principle had been excessively emphasized. Similarly, attachment to the money principle survived even when the industrial principle occupied the foreground. In short, it may be said that as English Mercantilism never consisted merely of an exaggeration of the value of the precious metals, so Protectionism, which is its later representative, has never wholly got rid of the anxious concern for a " favourable " money balance, which was a familiar mark of older Mercantilism.

So far as the influence of Mun is concerned, it would tend rather towards a shrewder or more enlightened view on some of the vexed economic questions of the time than that which was preached by some of his contemporaries and successors. Thus he seems to lay stress rather on a general overbalance on all the foreign trade than on a favourable balance in each specific case, and whilst there were many who condemned the East India Company because it carried bullion to the East and brought back only wares and little if any money, Mun pointed out that the wares were worth far more than the money sent out and that when exported to other countries in Europe, they brought. a balance of treasure to England.[19] Again, he recognized that the calculation of the assumed

5

balance was not so simple a matter as was often supposed, and he early had some notion of the rising activity and importance of banks and the growing significance of credit, which in time were to weaken the basis of Mercantilism.

The mercantilist writers always put forward as the aim of public policy the good of the commonwealth and the nation, and the need of subordinating the interests of individuals to those of the community. Economic questions were never considered by them in isolation, as a separate class of subjects, but were always envisaged in direct relation to the prosperity and power of the State. Yet even in mercantilist writers and still more in the practical policy of Mercantilism, the ostensible aim was commonly coloured or modified by the interests of persons, parties, corporations and classes. Indeed the government was often confronted by an almost impossible task in attempting to decide upon what interest it should favour or discourage for the benefit of the community, and even when purely national feeling found vent, it was frequently based upon a narrow and mistaken notion of what would contribute most effectively to the national welfare.

If English Mercantilism is witnessed at its best in the reign of Elizabeth, it is seen in certain of its more doubtful manifestations in the century which followed the Restoration, when the expansion of England was accompanied by an attempt to control the life of her dependencies upon the principles of an insular though not entirely selfish nationalism. The regulations which Charles I had been building up were elaborated into a system in the time of his son. The end of the revolutionary period brought an increased confidence which stimulated a revival of trade, and the development of Mercantilism now proceeded on a largely extended scale, not so much in the control of internal industry as in the spheres of foreign and colonial relations. National egoism asserted itself not simply as against foreign nations, but in dealings with the colonial offshoots of the nation and with the other parts of the British Isles.

The idea of an exclusive colonial policy was, as already remarked, by no means a new one. Carthage supplied an ancient precedent ; Venice had treated her dependencies on similar lines ; and the doctrine of the " sole market " inspired the colonial systems of Spain and France. In the second Navigation Act of Charles II it is declared to be a recognized custom " to keep the trade of one's plantations to one's self," and neither one power nor another was doing anything other than the usual thing, though they were not all doing it in exactly the same way, or with the same degree of intelligence, consistency, or thoroughness. The English Navigation Acts sought to confine the trade of the colonies to English or colonial ships and that with foreign countries to English or colonial vessels or ships of the country that produced the goods. The export of specified colonial products most wanted in England was forbidden, except to England, the trade of the colonies with Europe was severely restricted and controlled, and limitations were placed upon inter-colonial traffic. It was the aim of the system to encourage in the plantations the manufacture of only such goods and commodities as did not compete with English products and to maintain the colonies as markets for English goods. But it should be noted that if England endeavoured to preserve a " sole market " in the plantations, they were allowed a preferential market for their products in England, and in view of a common misapprehension it should be especially observed that the Navigation Acts did not in general discriminate against colonial shipping, for the term " English ships " was explained to cover vessels owned in the plantations, though the officers who had to administer the Acts sometimes put upon them the narrower interpretation.

The navigation policy of the seventeenth century was largely associated with the commercial rivalry between the English and the Dutch, which found more violent expression in the three Anglo-Dutch wars. It was the resentful belief of many of the Mercantilists, including Thomas Mun, that the prosperity of the Dutch was based mainly upon their fishing of the seas round Great Britain and Ireland, which were a veritable " gold mine " to the foreigners, and endeavours were made to stop the Dutch fisheries by revoking the licence and asserting the exclusive rights of the English over the " Narrow Seas "—a term which was somewhat broadly interpreted. But apart from this source of wealth, the enterprise of the Dutch had made them the great transporters of goods from country to country, and the Navigation Ordinance of 1651 and the Restoration Acts were especially directed against the Dutch carrying trade. •

It was long believed that this legislation was

primarily responsible for the decline of the Dutch power and the foundation of English maritime and commercial supremacy. But the evidence lends little support to this estimate of its practical significance. The Acts, though not perhaps the Ordinance, certainly succeeded in destroying to a large extent the Dutch trade with the colonies, though a good deal of illicit traffic still went on, but the loss in those regions seems to have stimulated the Dutch to increased energy in the Baltic trade, where England could not get a footing. Dutch shipping certainly did not suffer in bulk during the latter part of the seventeenth century, and its decline in the eighteenth is to be sufficiently explained by factors which were in operation apart from the working of the English Navigation Acts. Further, though a considerable enlargement of English shipping took place during the later seventeenth century, the inference that it was due to the protective legislation—which, be it noted, was very imperfectly carried out—rests upon little more than the notion that as shipping flourished the Acts must have done what they were intended to do, whereas the increase would rather seem to have been a specific illustration of a movement of English enterprise and expansion which had general causes not connected with the official navigation policy.[20]

If in one view the navigation law has figured as the " palladium of English prosperity," the " Charta Maritima," and the like, in another aspect it has been raised to a " bad eminence " as the leading cause of the loss of England's old colonial empire in North America. The American historian, Bancroft, wrote

that American independence, like the great rivers of
the country, had many sources, but the head spring
which coloured the streams was the Navigation Act.
John Adams [21] had declared that molasses was an
essential ingredient in American independence. Another ingredient assuredly was tea. But we have
to distinguish between general and remote causes on
the one hand, and particular and provoking causes on
the other. The investigation, extensive and intensive,
which the subject has undergone, has made it necessary
to abandon or modify many of the old ideas about it.
The general effect of the closer study is that more
allowance is now made for the motives and difficulties
of the English government, and more complexity is
now recognized in the causes of the revolt. Some of
the best work that has been produced in the direction of a fairer view has been done by American
scholars. [22]

The spirit of discontent, religious or political, that
drove many Englishmen across the Atlantic appears
to have flavoured the history of the plantations right
down to the time of revolution. [23] Its development,
under the influence of English ideas of self-government,
and under the conditions of life in the new land,
towards the spirit of American independence is clearly
traceable over a long period in the constant conflicts
between the provincial governors, standing for the
royal authority, and the assemblies, representing the
growing colonial self-consciousness, and this struggle
resulted in the establishment by the colonies, in some
cases, of a considerable degree of practical independence outside the letter of the law long before

the idea of formal and complete independence was conceived.[24]

So far as the actual working of the Mercantile Colonial System is concerned, it was neither so advantageous to England nor so harmful to the colonies as was formerly supposed. The machinery for enforcing it was altogether inadequate, and in many of its details the breach was more normal than the observance. Smuggling flourished, and it was only the profits of the illicit traffic that enabled the colonies to pay for the commodities imported from England. In spite of navigation laws and other measures, such as the Molasses Act, which, in the interest of English West Indian planters, aimed at preventing the continental colonies from exchanging their products for those of the French sugar islands,[25] the colonies worked up a large export trade to foreign markets, and got from them most of the European goods and tropical products that they required. New England shipping flourished, perhaps relatively more than that of old England, and colonial merchants made much gain and suffered little loss under the somewhat futile Mercantile System. It is questionable indeed whether the economic development of the colonies did not proceed much as it would have done without the ostensible restrictions.

It was the Seven Years War that transformed the practical situation and prepared the psychological way for revolution. England was called upon to protect her colonies against the French aggression, and the Mercantile Systems of the two countries came into sharpest collision in the west, as contemporaneously

in the east. But the habit of commerce with the
French was so firmly established that the English
colonies continued it during the war, thus trading
with the enemy, and supplying the French with
provisions which helped them to prolong the struggle.
England apparently triumphed in America as in
India, but the removal of the French danger, with the
conquest of Canada, by giving to the successfully
protected colonies a feeling of security, served only
to strengthen the urge of the American spirit towards
self-determination, though it was a very particularist
spirit, and as yet hardly knew exactly what it wanted,
whilst it was conscious of the benefits of the English
connexion so long as the colonial system could be
defied in its more restrictive parts. With this psychological trend in the colonies, the attempts of the
government to curb the degree of independence which,
as had recently been made obvious, the colonies had
already in practice achieved, to make the Mercantile
Sytsem more of a reality, and to secure what seemed only
reasonable, a colonial contribution through taxation
to the expenses of colonial defence, provoked a movement of protest which through a period of with-
drawals, reassertions, retaliations, agitations, hopes
and fears, passed into a civil war and then into a war
for independence.

Whatever the precise motives of the government
may have been, the attempt to enforce the Navigation
Acts appeared as an attack upon what was to the
colonies a necessary course of trade ; the putting of
the Molasses and Sugar Acts into execution was
resented as favouring the planters in the English

West Indies to the prejudice of the continental colonies ; other proceedings gave rise to the idea that the garrison for the upkeep of which taxation was demanded was intended not so much for the protection of the colonies as to prevent colonial expansion, out of fear lest expansion might lead to the development of economic independence ;[26] and the measure which allowed the East India Company the monopoly of the tea trade brought the reluctant colonial merchants into temporary and critically influential alliance with the extremists.[27]

It is impossible here to trace in detail the stages in the quarrel and show how mistakes on the part of the government helped the colonial radicals to an ascendancy over moderate and doubtful opinion. Many causes were at work in producing a struggle which had a simple result. With the aid of the French the colonies made good their independence. It is possible that without the French assistance they might have been defeated. It is possible also that in any case separation sooner or later was inevitable. But it is not inconceivable that a wiser policy, of which some men of the time had glimpses, might not only have averted the outbreak but have led the American spirit to a realization which was not incompatible with a maintenance of the English connexion, especially when improvements in transport and communication should have minimized the obstacle of distance.

The limited view of national interests which was common to all the leading powers in this age and which.was manifested by the English Parliament in its dealings with the colonies was also illustrated in its treatment of the other countries of the British Isles, and was one of the provoking causes of separatist movements in Scotland and Ireland.

Under the protectorate, the union with Scotland had been accompanied by commercial equality, and free trade prevailed between north and south Britain. The Restoration brought a return to the old political independence, and this was not unpopular, for the union had not been by consent ; but Scotland was now treated for the first time since the union of crowns as an alien economic nation.[28] The possession of a common monarch was of no avail to counteract the force of commercial antagonism. It is true that Scotland to some extent defied the prohibitions of the Navigation Acts in the matter of colonial trade. But her commerce was seriously restricted by them, whilst Scottish goods were more or less excluded from the English market. Scotland did not take this altogether " lying down." She had an independent Parliament, and attempted retaliation, but though English trade with Scotland suffered, the Scots reaped no advantage. English jealousy was notably displayed in relation to the Darien scheme. The bitterness of feeling thereby created amongst the Scots thwarted for a time all efforts at a closer union, and brought about a risk of complete separation and possibly war. It was the fear of such a catastrophe that enforced the advisability of a union whereby Scotland, while maintaining independent legal and religious systems, was admitted to commercial equality, to the ultimate advantage of both contracting parties.

But the most grievous sufferer under the English Mercantile System was Ireland,[29] and this fact contributed powerfully to the development of the formidable Irish question. The more rigorous application of the system to that country was due to obvious causes—religious, economic, political. She was not dominantly Protestant, like Scotland and America, but mainly Roman Catholic, and so was regarded with rooted suspicion by the English Parliaments. Again, her industrial possibilities were so similar to those of England as to provoke a peculiar jealousy amongst English manufacturers and merchants. Moreover, her Parliament was not an independent body, like the Scots, but since the enactment of Poynings' Law had been subordinate to the English Council, and even before the Declaratory Act of 1719 was regarded as subject to the overriding legislative power of the English Parliament. It thus did not possess even that small power of retaliation which the Scots Estates, in the days of independence, were able to exercise.

Something of the spirit of Mercantilism is seen in the measure by which Queen Elizabeth sought to confine Irish trade to those settlers in Ireland who were most devoted to her throne, but the real founder of Mercantilism in its application to Ireland was Wentworth. His work, which has already been noticed, was, however, purely administrative, and primarily in the interests of the Crown. After the Restoration, the economic subordination of Ireland to England was definitely adopted by Parliament itself. Under the Commonwealth, there had been no free trade between the two countries, but the Restoration found no Act on the statute, book which imposed restrictions on Irish industry and trade and placed duties on imports thence. There was soon commenced, however, a restrictive policy which, at first precautionary and afterwards both precautionary and punitive, was continued to the latter part of the eighteenth century. It is the more difficult to understand inasmuch as though Ireland suffered most, England also suffered, and probably no application of mercantilist principles in any other sphere illustrates so strikingly the inherent mischiefs of the system. As during the administration of Wentworth, the trade of Ireland was to be advanced, but only in such a way that it should not be prejudicial to England according to mercantilist conceptions. There was no envisaging of a common and united strength. The first Navigation Act of Charles I's reign, which linked Scotland with foreign countries, drew no distinction between English and Irish shipping, but that of 1663 ruled Ireland out of the economic unit so far as plantation trade was concerned. Ireland was definitely forbidden to export goods to the colonies, and by later Acts they were not to be exported to Ireland from the plantations. The general effect of these measures was the ruin of the Irish plantation trade; but on the other hand they had consequences which were by no means contemplated by Parliament. They caused the Irish to set up closer commercial relations with powers that were hostile to England—with France and Spain and their colonies. Another piece of legislation that had a similar twofold result was the famous Cattle Act, which forbade the importation of Irish cattle to England. A natural result was the sending up of the prices of beef in England, and though Ireland was robbed of her English market, she was stimulated to develop a trade in provisions and other commodities with foreign countries. Sheep runs began to replace cattle runs, and Irish wool sent abroad enabled continental competitors of England to undersell her in woollen manufactures whilst Irish provisions undersold English provisions abroad. Moreover, Ireland now tended to buy from other countries commodities which she had been wont to purchase in England. Her own woollen manufacture also developed considerably. In order to check this movement, an Act of 1698 forbade the export of Irish wool or woollens to any country except England—where the tariff itself afforded sufficient protection against the import of Irish cloth. The Irish trade was undoubtedly destroyed by the veto, but it is doubtful whether England did not lose by the embargo more than she might have lost by Irish competition, as one effect of the prohibition was a stimulus to emigration, and Irish wool-workers who went abroad helped the countries in which they settled so to develop their manufacture as to take from England much of her foreign trade. There were no obvious political advantages to compensate for the

of the policy on a reasonable c

English or Irish interests.

during the War of Americ

seemed to be a danger of

concessions were made in the

The Restoration period is marked by the establishment of French ascendancy in Europe—a consummation to which Cromwell by his alliance with Mazarin had undesignedly contributed ; and though Charles II himself was amicably inclined towards Louis XIV and became his pensioner, we find amongst the people generally a developing hostility towards France which after the Protestant Revolution was to work itself out in what Sir John Seeley called the second Hundred Years War with that country (1689–1815).   Alarm at the political and military aggressiveness of France on the Continent was reinforced by a realization of her far-reaching commercial and colonial designs, which ran counter to English claims and ambitions, and of what seemed to the mercantilist mind the patent fact that France was draining England of her gold.[30]   Early in Charles II's reign, it was pointed out that the commerce with France, which had greatly increased since the Cromwellian treaties, was eminently a " losing " trade, as the value of French imports vastly exceeded that of English exports, and a cry arose for the discouragement of the imports by the imposition of high duties.   Important as was the part played by the balance-of-trade doctrine in mercantilist policy, it was not, as we have seen, the only, or always the final, consideration.   Thus, commercial relations with Sweden were encouraged, though the trade was subjected, on the Swedish side, to severe mercantilist burdens, and was manifestly a " losing " one.   The determining object here for England was not " money," but " ships," for the great bulk of her naval materials came from the Swedish Baltic regions, and as yet could not well be obtained elsewhere. But in the case of the French trade, there was no such consideration to render the unfavourable balance tolerable to the English mercantilist. Matters were made worse when Colbert, the master mercantilist of the age, whose economic policy was directed largely against Dutch and English trade, introduced a tariff which practically closed the French market to the leading English goods. As the demand for some French commodities continued to grow, the disparity between exports and imports became wider still, and the mercantilist campaign was at length so effective that in 1678, on the ground that the wealth and treasure of the kingdom had been greatly exhausted by the importation and consumption of French commodities, an Act was passed which absolutely prohibited, for three years, the importation of the chief of these. This was not renewed by James II, but it was replaced by heavy duties on French imports. With the Protestant Revolution and the war with France into which England was thereby drawn, all commerce with France was forbidden. Thereafter the policies of prohibition and protection alternated according to the succession of war and peace or the ascendancy of the Whig or the Tory party, but even with the Tories in power, the Whig and mercantilist opposition was sufficient to wreck the proposal for a commercial treaty with the French which was proposed in connexion with the peace of Utrecht.

It was partly out of hostility towards France and to recoup England from another quarter for the loss which, as mercantilists believed, she was sustaining

through the French overbalance that attempts were
made to work up the trade with Portugal, where the
normal balance was as favourable to England as that
of the French trade was adverse.[31]   After her victory
in the war of 1653, the Commonwealth, here acting
in true mercantilist fashion, had used her strength to
impose upon Portugal a treaty which involved the
economic subordination of the weaker country.   The
relative positions of England and Portugal were just
the reverse to those of England and France.   Portugal
needed English goods, whilst, owing to her depressed
condition, she had little to send in return.   Thus the
balance of trade went strongly against her, and the
difference had to be paid for in bullion.   Whilst the
Portuguese looked upon English merchants as the
men that would ruin Portugal, English mercantilists
rejoiced in the Portuguese trade as providing a more
favourable balance than that with any other country.
Portugal sought to protect herself by prohibiting the
wearing of English cloths, but the French wars did
more towards improving the balance from her point
of view by making England more dependent upon
Portuguese wines.   It now appeared to England that
trade with Portugal might be developed at the expense
of France on a basis of mutual concession which
should yet be to the advantage of England.   French
wines had to be purchased with money, whereas
Portuguese wines might be procured with goods, and
the demand for Portuguese wines might be used to
secure a renewal of the demands for English cloths.
Hence the famous Methuen Treaty, which arranged for
the readmission of English cloths to Portugal, whilst

a preferential tariff was allowed to Portuguese wines coming to England.

The effects of this treaty have been the subject of much discussion and controversy. Adam Smith attacked it on the grounds that a preference was accorded by England but none by Portugal, that the capital artificially directed to the Portuguese trade might with advantage have been employed elsewhere, whilst it involved political complications with other countries.[32]   List, on the other hand, regarded it as a masterpiece of British commercial policy. It led, he says, to the exclusion of Dutch and Germans from the trade with Portugal and her colonies, reduced Portugal to a state of political dependence upon England, who acquired through this trade a supply of bullion which extended enormously her commercial intercourse with China and India, and thereby subsequently laid the foundation of her great Indian empire and enabled her to dispossess the Dutch from their most important trading stations.[33]   But List's appreciation of England's mercantilist policy tends to be somewhat inflated.   The treaty certainly increased her trade with Portugal, and both that country and Brazil became, as it were, commercial annexes of England.   It was a blow at both France and Holland, but to explain all the commercial development that followed the arrangement of the treaty as arising out of it is to take a manifestly exaggerated view of its effects, and when we set the loss against the gain, it is doubtful how far England really gained on the balance.   One effect of it was to destroy most of her trade with France, thus increasing the commercial

6

rivalry between the two countries, and generally intensifying and prolonging the hostile relations between them. Moreover, Portugal herself resented the English dominance and the over-balance, paid in Brazilian gold, in which English mercantilists rejoiced. Pombal, who declared war on English monopoly, succeeded in diverting part of the trade to France, and in improving native industry to some extent, and the measures adopted in assertion of the economic independence of Portugal were, at any rate, so far successful that when Adam Smith condemned the treaty he had much support in public opinion.[34]

The fact that the rivalry of England and France, which largely determined external relations during the eighteenth century—and with which the Methuen treaty, as we have seen, had a close connexion—was based mainly on colonial and commercial considerations, has helped to prompt the generalization that whereas earlier wars were wars of religion, those of the eighteenth century were due to commercial causes. This distinction has a superficial plausibility, but is much too clearly cut. There were economic motives at work in the earlier wars, and motives other than economic in the later. But it is none the less true that the interconnexion of war and trade under the old commercial system became particularly noticeable in the later seventeenth and the eighteenth centuries, so that the aspect of Mercantilism which was now emphasized was that in which the power of the State was employed in the active prosecution of the commercial interests of its nationals.[35] This is traceable more or less in the Dutch wars, in the wars of William III, the War of the Spanish Succession, the War of Jenkins' Ear, the War of the Austrian Succession, the Seven Years War, the War of American Independence, and the great French War. The fact that possessions were ordered and worked as " sole markets," so far as was possible, brought commercial and territorial aggressiveness into the channel of a common scheme of policy, and a necessary connexion was envisaged between the balance of trade and the balance of power, so that in this epoch, in Seeley's words, trade became " almost identical with war." [86]

It was at the Restoration that a definite tariff policy was inaugurated for the protection of English agriculture by the placing of high duties upon imports of foreign corn. Moreover, the Tories under Charles II started the practice, which under pressure from the landed interest was continued on a large scale by the Whigs at the Revolution, of granting a bounty on the export of corn when the home price stood below a certain minimum. The first Act seems to have helped, along with other causes, to stimulate export, though at the expense of a considerable drain upon the treasury. The effects of the Corn Bounty Act of 1689 have been much debated. By some it has been estimated as an eminently successful piece of mercantilist legislation, which contributed in a very important degree to English prosperity during the eighteenth century, especially in the stimulation of agriculture by steadying prices and securing a surplus for export in favourable, and at any rate a sufficiency for home consumption in unfavourable, years. But there is a lack of definite evidence as to its beneficial effects.   After it had been in operation for more than half a century there were complaints that it had failed to effect any of the objects which the mercantilists expected from it, and it is questionable whether it was at all responsible for increase in tillage, whilst it certainly did not lead to any enlargement in shipping.[37]   With the progress of the Industrial Revolution · and the rapid growth of the population, England ceased to be a corn-exporting country, and the protective corn laws, culminating in that of 1815, really did little for agriculture, though helping to keep up the price of food.

CHAPTER VI

HISTORY OF ENGLISH MERCANTILISM
III. DECLINE AND FALL

THE mercantilist doctrine dominated English economic policy until the latter part of the eighteenth century, but even before the end of the seventeenth some features of it were the subject of forcible attack.

Commercial jealousy, as already remarked, was especially directed against France, but it was mainly the Whigs who were hostile to that country and who prompted the policy that was predominant for nearly a century. The Tories, on the other hand, being less antagonistic to France, or even friendly to her, favoured a relaxation of the prohibitive or protective regulations that were enforced against her. In setting forth their considerations against the ruling attitude towards France, some of the Tory pamphleteers—Child, North, Barbon, and the rest—were moved to enunciate declarations concerning the character of international trade which seem like anticipations of the views subsequently put forward by Adam Smith.[1] Their arguments bore primarily upon the question of overbalance, and in particular they threw doubt upon the accepted position in regard to the balance of trade between England and France. They contended that the mere fact that imports from France to England exceeded

exports from England to France was no criterion as
to whether the French trade was or was not profitable
to England.   The point to consider was not the balance
of our trade with any particular country but the
general balance of our trade with all countries.   It
was, indeed, almost impossible to calculate the balance
between two given countries, whether from the
customs house returns or by any other means, and it
might be that though as between France and England
the balance might be adverse to us, the French trade
might be the occasion of commerce with other countries
that would be more to our advantage.   In point of
fact, the Tory pamphleteers in question did not
challenge the general theory of balance, but only
that of the necessity of maintaining a favourable
balance on the transactions with any given country,
and they did not get much beyond the best of Mun in
this connexion.   But in supporting their pleas, some
of them were drawn into making statements as to the
general character of trade and commerce which are
susceptible of a much broader interpretation than
that which they possibly intended to be put upon
them.   Thus in Barbon, we have a hint of the doctrine
that goods ultimately must pay for goods, and that if
we prohibit the importation of any foreign commodity,
we thereby limit the exportation of so much of the
native commodity as was wont to be exchanged for it.
North appears to hit hard at the policy of national
exclusiveness when he speaks of all the world as but
one nation in the matter of trade.   Though we must
endeavour not to read into these utterances more
than what was in the minds of the authors, they

undoubtedly point the way to the logical and consistent presentation of free trade ideas by Adam Smith.

At the same time practical developments were in progress that were sapping the foundations of the balance-of-trade doctrine so far as it aimed primarily at a money surplus, and indeed caused a shifting of the mercantilist emphasis to the importance of a favourable balance as a sign of the relative prosperity of home industry. The acquisition of treasure had seemed to be essential in the interests of national defence, but the growth of credit and the banking system, in which connexion the establishment of the National Debt and of the Bank of England are of high significance, rendered this consideration less urgent than it had previously been. Extraordinary expenditure was now met by loans, and the regulation of trade in such a manner as to produce an inflow of treasure became less apparently necessary. Moreover, as to another part of the system, the increasing spirit of enterprise and the expansion of England's markets induced a feeling that these could best be developed if all were allowed freedom to trade, rather than that certain areas should be left to the operation of regulated companies. Political factions, however, proved a strong obstacle in the way of the establishment of economic liberalism.

The changes effected by Walpole were generally in the direction of free trade, but he can hardly rank as a free trader in the now common sense of the term. He stands indeed midway between the mercantilist and the free trade positions.[2] His statement of 1721 has often been represented as an anticipation of the principles of *The Wealth of Nations*, but it really contains nothing that is not in accordance with mercantilist doctrine. It puts forward the aim of a favourable balance, and though it suggests a lowering of import duties on raw materials does not extend the proposal to those on manufactured goods—a very necessary part of modern free trade policy. Still the net result of his tariff reform was a removal of restrictions and thus an advance towards freedom of trade. In the colonial sphere, the policy of the typically mercantilist Molasses Act was later, as we have seen, to have serious consequences, but its enforcement was not attempted in Walpole's time, and though his colonial policy has received excessive praise yet, so far as it was one of non-interference, it was in the nature of a break with the old mercantilist ideas, and under him notable progress took place both in English and in colonial prosperity.

The British success in the Seven Years War owed much to the basis of material wealth which Walpole's policy had established. In the result, the range and security of British markets abroad were extended, and whatever advantages the old system of regulation and control may have possessed in earlier periods it certainly seemed now to require some modification in view of the enlarged possibilities that were open to British commercial enterprise. It was a failure at this juncture to read the signs of the times that precipitated the American revolt. Though there was really a complex of causes, what happened in America appeared above all to mark the failure of the old commercial system. Hence, though there was far from being a general conversion to modern free trade views, the appearance in the year of the Declaration of Independence (1776) of a treatise which presented a clearly reasoned attack upon the Mercantile System in all its aspects, and offered a simpler alternative, produced an impression which if not immediately and ideally effective helped to pave the way for a movement that within the next seventy years was to bring about a complete overthrow of the old order of national economic policy.

The Tory free traders had exercised some influence on the French Physiocrats,[3] who stand for the reaction in their country against the regime of Colbertism, and both Tory free traders and Physiocrats found an appreciative student in the author of *The Wealth of Nations*. But Adam Smith treated the subject with a completeness and cogency that win consideration if not always conviction in an eminent degree, and covered much ground that had not been adequately traversed before within the limits of a single comprehensive treatise.[4]

The wealth of nations, he urged, could be best secured when individuals were allowed to pursue their private interests unchecked. The less the State sought to control either domestic industry or international commerce, the better. Taxation, in particular, should be for revenue, not for control. He attacks the balance-of-trade theory with a force which prevented it from being urged again by any serious economist in anything like its old form, and exposed the exaggeration of the mercantilist notions concerning money and treasure. International trade, he pointed out, was a matter of mutual advantage. The idea that when two people or two nations traded one must gain and the other lose, and that the only way of gain is that by which exports exceed imports and so an overbalance is procured in money or treasure, was denounced as entirely fallacious. In point of fact each country gained by international trade, as each obtained what it wanted and got rid of the surplus which it did not want. It was a matter of comparative values. Moreover, there could not be anything in the nature of a permanent overbalance, as a country's exports must in time be paid for by its imports. The mercantilist view treated wealth as consisting in money, whereas the true wealth was money's worth. The balance that mattered was one not of exports over imports but of production over consumption, and this might exist even where there was no foreign trade at all. The various methods whereby it was sought to increase the country's wealth by ensuring a favourable balance and to promote English industry by regulation and control are subjected to a keen analysis. He examined and condemns the bounty system, the old colonial policy, the Irish industrial and commercial code, the system of regulated companies, the Methuen treaty and the restraints on trade with France, and lays down a golden rule of international trade that it is for the interest of a nation that neighbouring nations should be rich and not poor.

The vigour of Smith's onslaught on the Mercantile System—to which he gave the name—and his emphasis on the mutuality of international trade has led to a

twofold charge—of unfairness to the mercantilists
and an excessive cosmopolitanism. The mercantilists,
it is said, did not believe that money was the only
wealth ; they made no attempt to put forward a
system of economic policy ; and in many of the
expedients devised or adopted, economic considerations
were subordinated to political, and therefore are not
to be criticized, as Smith criticized them, as if they
belonged to a connected body of economic doctrine.[5]
This stricture is not without force, but though mercantilist teaching and practice were not consistently
systematic, they cannot be exempted from criticism
on the ground of the theoretical tendencies and the
economic results which they involved. The effectiveness of Adam Smith's handling of Mercantilism on
this basis cannot be denied, nor can it be denied that
he frequently shows the futility of mercantilist
expedients even from the standpoint of national
power. That Adam Smith's teaching that the doctrine
of free trade in general tends in the direction of cosmopolitanism need not be disputed, nor is such a
judgment necessarily a condemnation ; but cosmopolitanism in Adam Smith, whatever may have been
the case with some of his followers, is not inconsistent
with a very strong national sentiment, which has been
strangely ignored by many of those who have attacked
him in this particular. Thus, while he condemns the
Navigation Acts on economic grounds he justifies
them on political grounds, for defence, he remarks,
" is of more importance than opulence." Indeed,
he credits them in this connexion with an effect which
is not clearly apparent on the evidence. To read

cosmopolitan doctrine into the title of Adam Smith's work [6] is obviously illegitimate, and he lays it down clearly that the great object of the political economy of every country is to increase the riches and power of that country. But his conception of the matter had a far broader basis than that of the Mercantilist, as is seen in his scheme of Imperial Federation. His project of a customs union, be it noted, was not accompanied by any plan of preferential tariffs. [7]

The greatest contemporary student of *The Wealth of Nations* was the younger Pitt, who came into office immediately after the definite loss of the old American colonies had practically discredited the narrow conception of national interests which Smith had made the object of his main attack. He was not only a student but a disciple, and in his years of peace made considerable progress in reforming the economic policy of England in the direction to which Smith had pointed in his treatise. Pitt reduced the duties on various articles of common consumption and sought to remove restrictions in all the main spheres of foreign trade in regard to which Smith had condemned the existing regime. Thus he attempted but in vain to carry a measure for the establishment of free trade between England and Ireland. He wished to offer full freedom of trade to the United States. This proved impossible, but it was found impracticable to continue the strict enforcement of the Navigation Acts so far as the States were concerned, and it was eventually relaxed so as to allow the people of the old American colonies to export to England in their own ships. A proposal from France, whose economic policy had become comparatively liberal, that the two powers in conjunction with the other powers should abolish all exclusive trade fell through, but a few years later Pitt was able to carry a commercial treaty with France on the principle of mutual concessions.[8] By this agreement French wines were to be allowed to come to England on the same scale of duties as that at which Portuguese wines were admitted. The Methuen treaty, as we have seen, was not working satisfactorily, and no objection to the British treaty with France was raised on behalf of Portugal. It was Pitt's main object, by this more liberal trade policy, to promote more friendly relations between France and England, and in commending it to Parliament he strongly protested against the mercantilist doctrine of inevitable international antagonisms. Portugal, it may be noted, was able to equalize matters by the supply of cotton from Brazil to meet the requirements of the growing English manufacture.

There had been general anticipations that the loss of the American colonies would involve a corresponding loss of the growing trade between England and America. But the needs of the new Republic brought about a contrary result, and the political loss to England was thus followed by economic gain, an apparent contradiction to that element in Mercantilism which connects political with economic power. This fact had a powerful effect in helping to bring home to men the wisdom of Smith's teaching. But it was the momentous series of changes known as the Industrial Revolution that worked the final overthrow of the Mercantile System. The greatest of the old trades, that of wool, had suffered much under what was intended to be the protective policy of the State. The new staple, cotton, grew up without any favour from the Crown, and the enterprise of the new manufacturing class which now arose in various industries began to feel mercantilist restrictions as shackles, hampering the free play of the new forces that had been brought into existence. The great French war helped to prolong the reign of Mercantilism, but when the worst effects of it were beginning to be worked off, the free trade movement began to make headway, representing the economic aspect of that growth of liberalism which is a distinguishing feature of the third decade of the nineteenth century. The theories which had been advanced by Adam Smith and other economists were now pressed upon the government by the commercial classes themselves, and the petitions of the London merchants and the Edinburgh Chamber of Commerce in 1820 set forth in clear and unmistakable fashion the principles of free exchange and the disadvantages of the protective system.[9] The numerous prohibitive and restrictive duties of our commercial system, it was pointed out, operated as heavy taxes upon the community at large without bringing any appreciable benefit to the classes in whose favour they had been instituted. Moreover, they had provoked similar impositions on the part of other countries, especially directed against England. A committee appointed by the House of Commons to inquire into the subject produced a report which fully confirmed the contentions of the petitioners, and recommended a gradual approximation to a free trade system as the standard of future commercial policy. The example of England, it was said, had helped to stimulate and keep up a protective policy in other countries. Her pre-eminence and prosperity had been ascribed to her policy of exclusion and restriction. This was a mistaken notion, for her commercial greatness and maritime power were due to the combined working of a free constitution and the enterprise of her people, and if England took the lead in the matter of free trade, her action would doubtless be potently effective in aiding the general progress towards the establishment of a liberal and enlightened system of national intercourse throughout the world.

The movement gathered force increasingly. But it is well to remember that the freeing of trade was not a sudden new departure. The old system had been modified in one respect after another even before the close of the great French war. The Navigation Laws had been partially repealed so far as the United States and Brazil were concerned. The Statute of Apprentices had been repealed, and other laws regulating trade and industry had fallen into desuetude. The new commerce and manufactures introduced by the Industrial Revolution had risen to vigour without that government control and protection which had been applied to the older trades, and unregulated commercial companies were growing up. But the movement now took on a determined offensive, and the next generation witnessed the overthrow of the Mercantile System and the establishment of free trade by the legislative achievements of Huskisson, Peel and Gladstone. The name of Huskisson is specifically associated with the introduction of the reciprocity principle into the Navigation Laws, which later were entirely repealed. That of Peel is connected particularly with the abolition of the Corn Duties, which had been the last expression of the spirit of Mercantilism in English legislation, and had had the effect not only of keeping up the price of food but of restricting the market for English products abroad. Each of the three ministers named had a hand in the reform of the general tariff by reduction or abolition in such a way as to set up the principle of taxation for revenue, not protection or control. But the brunt of the campaign for free trade was borne by Cobden, Bright, Villiers, and other unofficial reformers.[10]

Few serious students of economic history doubt the wisdom of the liberating movement at the time when it was carried out. Indeed, List, one of the ablest critics of unconditional free trade, believed that it would have been to the advantage of England to inaugurate the policy sooner, though he held that in commending the same procedure to other countries England was studying her own interests rather than theirs. But List seems to have failed to make sufficient allowance for the appreciation in England at this period of free trade doctrine as a general principle. However that may be, the result of the revolution in economic policy which the Industrial Revolution had really necessitated was a large increase in British industry and commerce. The repeal of the Navigation Acts, so far from proving the death of the Mercantile Marine, was followed by a considerable expansion of British shipping. The new agricultural policy stimulated amongst owners and farmers an enterprise which afforded proof that agriculture could flourish without protection ; and the general volume of trade swelled enormously. It is important that we should not exaggerate the extent of this expansion, or give to it any " single cause " explanation. Much of the rise in import and export values was due to the increase in prices consequent upon the discovery of the Californian and Australian gold mines, which necessarily lessened the buying power of money, and other factors contributed their shares in the development. But when all allowances have been made, the fact of progress is undoubted, and when we examine the conditions which helped to build up the new prosperity it is impossible to avoid the conclusion that the abandonment of mercantilist State regulation and control was one of the most significant causes.

The history of the Mercantile System nowhere else presents so continuous and completed a development as in England, but its development there was necessarily influenced and modified by political and economic tendencies and movements in other countries. Indeed, the long maintenance of English Mercantilism was only rendered possible by the comparative moderation with which it was applied and the prudence with which its rigour was relaxed in face of competitive or conflicting forces. It was remarkably distinguished from the pursuit of a theory to its extreme which has characterized the economic policy of some other nations. Yet it has produced a strong impression, which has taken the shape now of retaliation, now

7

of simple imitation, both in the Old world and in the New, and not least upon the nations which have established or unified themselves in and since the period of its decline and fall—upon the United States, upon Germany, upon Japan. It may thus be said that during the past century, in the sphere of economic policy, the historical example of England, whether rightly or wrongly interpreted, has had more weight with rising powers than her contemporary example has had. It is proposed to notice in subsequent chapters the main features of the mercantilist movement in the countries other than England where it has been most definitely marked.

CHAPTER VII

HISTORY OF EUROPEAN MERCANTILISM —SPAIN, PORTUGAL, THE NETHERLANDS

IF English Mercantilism showed, on the whole, more balance and moderation than were displayed in the systems of other countries, the vices of incoherence and excess are most conspicuously exhibited in the economic policy of Spain during the greater part of the same period.

It was in the Iberian peninsula that the Mercantilism of the territorial State first made its appearance, for as far back as the thirteenth century some of its features are to be traced in the policy of James I of Aragon ; but it was not till the reigns of Ferdinand of Aragon and Isabella of Castile, who by their marriage and the conquest of Granada brought the whole of the peninsula, except Portugal, under their rule, that the building up in Spain of a national economy, under monarchic control, could be definitely undertaken. An all-round development of the resources of the country was doubtless contemplated by these mercantilist rulers, but the course taken by Spanish enterprise in relation to the other world pool with other factors to produce something different kind.

The discovery of the We up of central and south Ar

empire which was rich in the precious metals that were so much wanted in Europe and this determined the main lines upon which the economic policy of the Spanish rulers should henceforth proceed. Portugal and Spain were the pioneers in the modern application of the old idea of an exclusive colonial empire simply because Portugal in the East and Spain in the West led the way in distant acquisitions. That Spain was the beginner on a large scale of that exaggerated Mercantilism which looked upon treasure as the pre-eminent form of wealth was due to the simple fact that the territories which she was able to annex abounded in silver and gold. The balance-of-trade systems, whereby other countries sought to retain or attract a goodly supply of the precious metals, and the bullionist regime of Spain, whereby she endeavoured to monopolize the treasures of the western mines, were equally products of the mercantilist spirit, operating in different sets of circumstances, and acting and reacting one upon another.

The ruling principle of the Spanish, as of other colonial systems, was to control the development of the dependencies in the interests of the metropolitan power. Industry in the colonies was limited, as far as possible, to the exploitation of the mines, which were worked by native and slave labour. The administration was placed in the hands of Spanish-born officials, and colonial commerce and industry alike were subjected to minute regulation. The carrying trade was confined to royal vessels, and foreigners were forbidden to traffic with the Spanish possessions. The main object of the restriction of colonial industry was on the one hand to secure a concentration upon the mines, and upon the other to make the colonies dependent upon Spanish manufactures and commodities, which would thus be able to command monopoly prices. The extent to which colonial industry was discouraged has, however, usually been somewhat exaggerated, as even occupations that were similar to those of the mother country were not always or uniformly vetoed, whilst it should be added that recent research has led to some modification of the views that were formerly held as to the ruthless exploitation and oppression to which the natives and the negroes were exposed, and also to the conclusion that on the whole Spanish America was probably not governed any worse than was Spain herself. [1]

It was hoped that by the procurement of treasure direct from the mines and by the profits obtained from the colonial demand for European goods and commodities, the power of Spain would be firmly rooted in the enjoyment of abundant wealth. In order to retain treasure in the country, not only was its carrying out prohibited, in accordance with earlier policy, but it was ordered that such foreign goods as were bought should be paid for with Spanish products, and not with Spanish money. But the system failed to produce anything other than an artificial appearance of wealth and power. The colonial monopoly for a time gave a stimulus to industry, but the influx of the precious metals had the effect for a considerable period of sending up prices in Spain to a level beyond that reached in other countries, as the veto on transportation checked any movement of equalization.

Moreover, the lust for treasure gained strength at the expense of industrial enterprise, and the monopolist policy provoked attacks, in the way of smuggling and buccaneering—wherein the Elizabethan seamen especially distinguished themselves—which involved much loss to Spain. The wars on this account, and arising out of the Hapsburg holdings and connexions of her rulers, involved heavy taxation which had ruinous effects upon the economic life of Spain.

Commerce, industry, and agriculture alike were stifled by over-regulation, often by measures specifically intended for their protection or promotion, and the century which saw the climax of Spanish splendour saw her with a declining population. Early in the next century, the backbone of both agriculture and industry in Spain disappeared with the expulsion of the Moriscoes. The Castilian gild of sheep owners, known as the Mesta, which regarded with jealousy the agricultural activities of the Moriscoes, seems to have had some share in the movement against them. The development of agriculture in Spain was stunted for centuries by the favour accorded to the Mesta by her kings. The royal action in this regard was determined by the consideration that the merino wool from the Mesta sheep was the most important Spanish commodity with which foreign gold could be procured, or which could be exchanged for necessary foreign commodities, but the privileges granted to the gild bore hardly on both town and country districts where their nomadic flocks were authorized to pasture, and especially on sedentary husbandry.

With the decline of industry and agriculture, Spain

found herself increasingly dependent upon foreign sources of supply and, not having goods wherewith to pay for goods, had to pay out her treasure. Moreover, the wars in which she engaged, particularly when maintaining armies composed of strangers, involved a large expenditure of money outside the kingdom. The bullionist Mercantilism of Spain was strongly condemned by balance-of-trade Mercantilists, and Thoman Mun devotes a special chapter of his treatise to the thesis that the Spanish treasure cannot be kept from other kingdoms by any prohibition in Spain. " That country," he remarks, " by war and want of wares doth lose that which was its own."

The policy pursued by Spain in regard to her possessions in the West had been paralleled by the colonial system of Portugal in the East and in Africa, except that treasure from mines was not there similarly in question. The exclusive commercial regime of Portugal was indeed largely responsible for the decline which had already taken place in her empire when, in 1580, she was annexed to the crown of Spain, and the whole of the enlarged Spanish empire fell under one scheme. The policy of monopoly thereafter led to vigorous attack from both the English and the Dutch, and most of the Portuguese colonies were lost during the period of Spanish rule. In 1640 Portugal again became an independent kingdom, but she had no longer a great empire, and the sixty years of servitude to Spain were followed by a much longer period, in which, under the system that found its culminating expression in the Methuen Treaty, the economic interests of Portugal were subordinated to those of mercantilist England, though it is doubtful whether any advantage thus gained by England was not more than counterbalanced by the exacerbation of her relations with France. In later times the economic progress of Portugal has been greatly hindered by her own restrictive system.

In the meanwhile, by the end of the seventeenth century, not only had Spain lost the Portuguese possessions, but her colonial and foreign commerce had been practically ruined. Industry and agriculture alike were in the most languid condition, and vagrancy and indolence prevailed. Her position was in marked contrast with the colonial and commercial activity of England, France, and Holland. It was the War of the Spanish Succession, which brought the Spanish throne and possessions into the hands of a member of the French house of Bourbon, that led to an attempt to revive Spanish prosperity by an industrial and commercial system such as that which had been adopted by Colbert in France in the first part of the reign of Louis XIV.

The movement found its leading literary advocate in Uztariz, the first Spaniard to put forward a system of political economy.[2] Uztariz urged a systematic endeavour to organize the forces of production, regulate the organization of labour, and distribute products on the lines of a wider Mercantilism than that of the bullionist theory. He did not altogether abandon bullionism, but he preached the virtues of a balance of trade which was to be ensured by the development of industry. He had studied carefully the economic policies of England, Holland, and France, and advocated the introduction into Spain of measures on the same lines but adapted to the special needs of his country. He pointed to the English Navigation Acts in regard to shipping, and above all to the Colbert regime with reference to customs and manufactures. Like other mercantilists he saw in the direct protection of industry by the State the principal source of national prosperity. His aim was to establish the economic independence of Spain, and it has been said that in his conception of an organized national economy he may be regarded as the precursor of the school of which the German List is the most distinguished representative.[3]

Under Philip V and his successors the reform of the Spanish economic system on these lines was definitely undertaken. Whilst the examples of England and Holland were not without effect, it was that of France which prevailed and predominated. In short, Spanish Mercantilism of the eighteenth century was simply a copy, so far as possible, of the Colbert system—a system of comprehensive government control and protection. Royal manufactures were established, privileges granted to private establishments, and industry generally subjected to detailed regulation. It was sought to encourage exports by reducing tariffs, discourage imports of foreign manufactures by high customs dues, and promote commerce by the establishment and encouragement of privileged companies. The conveyance of Spanish products was to be reserved to Spanish vessels. The system included elements which made it superior to the narrow bullionist regime which it supplanted and had an undoubted effect in the stimulation of industry and commerce, but the revival was forced and artificial, and proved only temporary. It shared the defects of the regime which it imitated. Thus attention was concentrated on manufactures to the neglect of agriculture, after the manner of Colbert, though not after the fashion of English Mercantilism, and the policy of subsidy and privileged companies had very mixed results. The imposition of an industrial system from above was not effective in eradicating the indolence and lack of power of concentration which had been induced amongst the people by the bullionist policy. The movement culminated in the reign of Charles III, whose minister, Campomanes,[4] however, shows the influence both of Colbert and of the Physiocrats, and who did a good piece of work by giving the Mesta what was practically its death-blow, though it did not finally disappear till many years afterwards. The success of the reform did not long survive Charles III. It depended too much upon the ability of the king and his ministers, and when these failed the new industrial and commercial life tended to die down.

The dynastic link with France as well as her own jealousy of England led Spain to intervene on the side of the Americans in the war which resulted in the loss to England of her older colonies in North America —the first great blow to her Mercantile System. England, in turn, and her former colonies were to assist by their power and policy, though not by arms, in the loss to Spain of her vast empire in Central and South America. The colonial system of Spain had been greatly modified in the period which we have been considering. The colonial trade had been thrown open to all Spaniards, and intercolonial trade was permitted, and this more liberal policy was accompanied and followed by a considerable increase in the commerce with the colonies. But it was futile so far as one of its main objects was to keep out the foreigner, and it was too late to counteract the effects of the long period of restriction. The Mercantile System proceeded on the assumption that political control of a colony gave the nation controlling it the right to exclusive exploitation, and in Latin America only a favourable occasion was required to stimulate the spirit of revolt into activity with the hope of throwing off political and economic control alike. It was the intervention of Napoleon in Spain and the disturbance thereby created that furnished the opportunity for insurrection, and when the Peninsular War was in progress Mexico was in revolt against the tyranny of the Spanish viceroy, the leading grievance apparently being the manner in which, despite formal concessions, commercial and other privileges were reserved for the Spanish-born residents. This was the beginning of a movement which resulted in the loss to Spain of the whole of her continental American possessions, and to Portugal of Brazil, and the formation of a number of new States in Latin America.[5]

The economic progress of Spain after the loss of the colonies was for a long time hampered by constitutional and other domestic troubles, and by her exceptionally prohibitive commercial regime. A modification of this system during the period when free trade ideas had some vogue in Europe had beneficial results, but the tariff was still restrictive in character, and with the increase of international competition Spain took part in the neo-mercantilist movement towards increased protection which it engendered. Thus the French tariff of 1892 led to Spanish retaliation. An artificial spur was given to industry, but the rate of commercial progress was checked. During the World War Spain profited much as a neutral, but the collapse of the war and post-war boom, due chiefly to the revival of industry in the formerly belligerent countries and renewed competition, provoked a cry for a " super-tariff " in the interests of national production, and brought on a customs war with France which temporarily did considerable injury to the relations between the two countries. The ruling scale is much more than double that which ruled before the war.

Affairs in Spain are at present in a somewhat disturbed condition, but her natural resources are so great that with a freer industrial and commercial regime she could look forward to a prosperity far more stable and substantial than that which attended her in the days of her most conspicuous political power.

In the century of Spain's ascendancy the attempt of Philip II to establish a centralized Spanish despotism in his Hapsburg heritage of the Netherlands led to the breaking away of the northern provinces from his dominion. During the period of their revolt and in the first generation of their practical independence the Dutch succeeded in building up a commercial power that equally evoked the admiration and provoked the jealousy of other countries—a double effect which is amply evidenced in the pamphlet literature and the national policies of the time.[6]

Holland possessed comparatively little natural wealth, but her people set themselves with remarkable resolution to the exploitation of such resources as were open to them. They developed both agriculture and manufacture, but gave their main attention to shipping and the carrying trade—a direction in which it was especially turned by the character of their geographical environment—and the course thus taken by their most vigorous enterprise determined the form that Mercantilism assumed amongst them. Though they had risen against oppression, the Dutch shared in the monopolist ideas of the age, and the spirit of exclusiveness is clearly reflected in their industrial and commercial systems during this epoch. The restrictions to which industry was subjected were perhaps more mediaeval than modern, representing the Mercantilism of the gild or city rather than that of the nation, and with the growing predominance of commerce—a traffic which was only to a relatively small extent in Dutch products—the tariff wall was kept comparatively low in order to admit the goods and commodities that Holland did not herself supply. But the Mercantilism of the Dutch as a nation fell in no wise behind that of others in the rigorous measures which they employed to the end of keeping to themselves the trade of the distant dependencies that their maritime and commercial adventures had secured for them. In some colonies they also adopted the common mercantilist rule of prohibiting occupations that might compete with home manufactures, and they had the common concern for bullion.

The Dutch made themselves the great carriers of commerce between country and country, and between the Old World and the New, and the wealth acquired by trade enabled them to show the way in banking and other financial operations. Their predominance, which became strikingly obvious during " the golden age of Frederick Henry " in the second quarter of the seventeenth century, was unshaken to the beginning of the eighteenth, the English Navigation Acts having failed to prevent a continual increase of their traffic. The War of the Spanish Succession, however, hit Dutch commerce hard, and within the next generation Holland yielded place to England and France.

How is her decline to be explained ? It has often been attributed to a want of completeness in her Mercantile System. We have been told that she lacked and did not seek to create, a consolidated political power, without which commercial supremacy could not be long sustained ; that she fell a victim to her own free trade and the aggressive protectionism of the strong political powers of England and France ; and that she made the mistake of basing her prosperity upon the shifting foundation of commerce rather than the firm foundation of manufactures.[7]

Now, there can be no doubt that particularism was a well-marked feature amongst the Dutch cities and provinces, that they failed to establish a really unified

State, and that Holland suffered at the hands of great political powers; but we have seen that the most famous of the protective expedients directed against her—the English Navigation Acts—caused no decrease in Dutch shipping, and the suggestion that Holland was injured by such degree of free trade as she allowed is singularly unconvincing. An increase of prosperity was the usual sequel to any relaxation of her rigid colonial regime, and Dutch industries seem to have been hampered rather by the presence of gild and city restrictions than by the absence of tariff protection. The criticism of Holland on the ground that she over-specialized in shipping and commerce—for which she was peculiarly fitted—rests to some extent upon an exaggerated estimate of the part which manufactures play in the economic healthfulness of a nation,[8] and the Dutch certainly did not fail in shipbuilding—the manufacturing industry which in their case could be most profitably pursued. Wars, heavy taxation, due partly to wars and partly to the artificial and therefore expensive character of Holland's geographical make-up, gild restrictions, excess of the monopolist spirit in their trading companies, a diminution of new enterprise amongst the Dutch, and the increase of competition—these are patent causes of their decline. The governmental factor was undoubtedly of high importance in connexion with them, but its significance has been over-emphasized. On the one hand, the energy of the Dutch won for them extraordinary success without the aid of a strong political organization, and on the other, whatever might have been the form and force of their government, and apart from the contributory causes mentioned above, the overwhelming preponderance of the Dutch was bound to be overthrown sooner or later with the progress of other nations. The decline of Holland, however, was not her ruin, and though she had further troubles to pass through she was to experience a return of prosperity under a free trade regime.

During the great French war Holland was brought into subjection to the French. At the peace, it was her desire to essay the work of restoration on a free trade basis, but the union with Belgium involved Holland in a protective system.[9] This was not to her advantage, but protective tariffs, once set up, were maintained for many years after the dissolution of the union. The free trade movement, however, gained ground. In the 'sixties it made its way into the tariff, where it reached its culminating point in 1877. There has been variation since then, but the economic progress of Holland under free trade has been such that the system has not been seriously disturbed. With the neo-mercantilist movement in other countries, and the depression of Dutch agriculture in the 'eighties, a demand for agricultural protection arose, but the fact that agriculture in protectionist countries was not obviously faring better than in Holland ensured the failure of the campaign, and the flourishing state into which agriculture has been brought with the progress of co-operation amongst the farmers has caused the demand for agricultural protection to disappear from Dutch protectionist propaganda, which in late years has been concentrated on the idea of protection in the interest of national manufacture.

Belgium, mainly a manufacturing nation, returned, after an interval of liberal tariffs, to a protectionist policy, but has found it necessary to pursue it with much caution and moderation.

CHAPTER VIII

HISTORY OF EUROPEAN MERCANTILISM
—FRANCE

THE wars of England, France, Spain, and Holland were a necessary outgrowth of the prevailing mercantilist aim and practice, in which political and economic considerations were always closely associated. Mercantilist expedients or experiments in one country often stimulated or provoked similar measures in another, and the spirit of retaliation easily passed into or became merged in that of military opposition. The most notable illustration of the resolute application of mercantilist principles, if we consider equally its essential features and its influence on the economic policy of other countries, is supplied by the commercial and industrial history of France.

The territorial and political unification of France under the Crown was not completed until the early sixteenth century, and the development of her economic unity was an even slower process.[1] It is perhaps in the reign of Philip the Fair, in the fourteenth century, that we find the real beginning of the attempt to establish a national and monarchic economic policy which should supersede or subordinate to itself the more or less independent economies of the seigneurs and the towns. The regime which he set up was eminently protective, prohibitive, and restrictive in character, and had its share in producing the circumstances that provoked the outbreak of the Hundred Years War. Under the monarchs of the period of restoration after that war—the founders of the " New Monarchy " in France—the royal economic policy alternated between greater freedom and greater rigour on somewhat empirical lines, and it has to be said that right down to the seventeenth century it was to a large extent more formal than practically effective. Edicts were often issued which were carried out only very partially or not at all, and declarations made which remained merely pious opinions, because edicts and declarations assumed in France a degree of economic unity which did not really exist.

The Wars of Religion, however, led to the enthronement of a spirit which subordinated all the interests of French society to the one aim of national power. Bourbon Mercantilism, following upon the Wars of Religion, furnishes an interesting parallel to Tudor Mercantilism, following upon the Wars of the Roses. During the Wars of Religion, France had become dependent upon England for her supplies of many things. Towards the close of the century this dependence began to be resented, and Henry IV and his ministers, in the establishment of civil peace, addressed themselves to the foundation of the economic independence of their country.

Whilst allowing for previous traces and tentatives of the same spirit, we may well regard the paternal government of Henry IV in the sphere of economic policy as the first clear realization of Mercantilism in France. But it is necessary to make some discriminations in this matter. Inasmuch as in this reign a definite attempt was made to increase the wealth and power of the State by government control and regulation of agriculture, industry, and commerce, the policy pursued was clearly mercantilist. But if Sully is to be taken as a mercantilist statesman he can only be described as a mercantilist with a difference. Whilst he introduced sweeping and effective reforms in the finances, he had no share in the mercantilist exaggeration of the value of bullion, to which the rival power of Spain was especially prone. The real mines of France, he said, were husbandry and pasture. As we have seen, an emphasis on the food supply as an element in national power always formed an important part of English Mercantilism, but it is often said that Sully, in concentrating his attention on the encouragement and development of agriculture and comparatively neglecting the promotion of manufactures, was in some sort a precursor of the Physiocrats of the eighteenth century rather than a typical representative of mercantilist doctrine. There is reason to think, however, that somewhat exaggerated inferences and conclusions have been drawn from Sully's expressions and proceedings in this connexion. But whatever view we may take of Sully, the mercantilist doctrine found vigorous propagandists in the Laffémas, father and son, and in the policy which Henry himself pursued with little support from his minister. Bartholomew Laffémas pressed the conception of the economic unity of the State and advocated thorough government control both of industry and of commerce on definite mercantilist lines—the exclusion of foreign goods and the stimulation of home industries. He especially urged the planting of mulberry trees and the breeding of silkworms to the end of establishing a silk manufacture and forbidding the importation of silks from abroad. The actual attempts of Henry to promote the cultivation of silk were, however, unsuccessful; and though on the whole there was an undoubted economic revival in France during this reign, it is arguable that it was rather due to the peace which prevailed after the wars of the previous century, the general financial reforms which were effected, and the removal of many restrictions on internal trade and, in the case of grain, on exportation, than to any measures of direct control and restriction.

The next great minister of France—in some respects the greatest in her history—Richelieu, carried on the mercantilist spirit.[2] In the sphere of trade and commerce, as in that of the general administration, government control was exercised with a strong hand. Richelieu paid special attention to the development of commerce and shipping. He encouraged the growth of a mercantile marine and forbade the exportation of French merchandise in foreign vessels. He sought to promote colonization and entrusted colonial enterprise entirely to exclusive companies. But, whilst many of his measures may certainly be counted for progress, it cannot be said that his economic policy generally was remarkably successful. Excessive dependence upon State patronage was largely responsible for the failure of the companies. Both agriculture and industry suffered through the system of close and privileged corporations which prevailed and the continuance of internal customs which it had been Sully's aim to sweep away. The excessive centralization introduced by Richelieu in France and his neglect of financial reform were largely responsible for the reaction and revolution that were to bring to an end the strong monarchy which it was his main object to establish.

But the greatest of French mercantilists, and perhaps the most notable of all mercantilist statesmen, is Colbert, whose name has supplied one of the alternative titles of the Mercantile System.[1]

It was Colbert's aim to set up a complete system of industrial and commercial control in the interests of national power. He came into office at a time of financial confusion and general economic depression in France, and determined to lay the foundations of a flourishing national commerce as the only true method of revival. France was to be entirely self-sufficing. By the establishment or re-establishment of industries she was to be made independent of strangers for all necessaries. There was nothing especially new in the methods of Colbert—practically all of which had been set forth by Laffémas in his proposals ⸺ but he applied them with an almost unprecedented energy and thoroughness. The system was one of rigorous control applied by an almost absolute royal power. Attempts were made to stimulate forestry and mining, but it was found impossible to produce within the realm all the raw materials that its industries required. Hence imports of these were allowed at a comparatively low tariff, and main attention was paid to the promotion of manufactures, in contrast to the policy of Sully, who had been interested chiefly in the development of agriculture. Privileges, subsidies, and bounties were granted to individuals and corporations for the setting up of new manufactures, and the details of production were the subject of minute government regulation. Tariffs within the kingdom were reduced or abolished, as these tended to restrict the internal traffic which Colbert sought to promote. To this extent Colbert was a domestic or inter-provincial free trader, and pointed the way to an ideal of fiscal unity which was not to be completely realized till the time of the French Revolution. For the protection of home industries, however, heavy tariffs or actual prohibitions were imposed upon the importation of manufactured goods. But whilst Colbert endeavoured to render France independent of foreign wares, an external outlet as well as the home market for French products was seen to be necessary. Hence export duties on manufactured goods were brought to a minimum. His policy in this connexion was dictated by the mercantilist doctrine of the balance of trade, the conception of which does not appear to have been definitely formulated in France before his time. The power of a nation, he declared, depended solely upon the abundance of money within the State, and trade must be so directed as to secure a money surplus on transactions with other countries. Like other observers, he was greatly impressed by the history of Spain, and the amazing apparent power of her rulers during the sixteenth century. Colbert seems to have attributed this expansion primarily to the treasure which flowed into her coffers through the discovery of the Indies ; and to the end that France might conserve her supplies of the precious metals, an embargo was placed upon the export of gold and silver. But though he overestimated the treasure of the West as a factor in the power of Spain, he recognized, as English Mercantilism recognized, the mistake which Spain had made in neglecting industry. It was from French industry and its surplus products that by foreign trade an accumulation of national wealth was to be obtained. Foreign trade, however, could, he believed, only be increased at the expense of other countries, and he therefore endeavoured to push it especially at the expense of the English and the Dutch, the most enterprising peoples of the age. Colbert's tariffs affected both, and the chartered companies which he established were primarily designed to oust the Dutch from the extra-European trade. He laboured to shut out both them and other foreigners from the profits of commerce with the colonies of France, from which at the beginning of his ministry the home country was receiving little benefit.

Colbert's colonial policy was purely mercantilist in its object and methods. The interests of the colonies were definitely subordinated to those of the motherland, and their one *raison d'être*, in the official view, was to provide an ever-increasing commerce for France. They were to constitute markets for her manufactures and for whatever her traders might bring to them, whilst they were to furnish raw materials for her industries or for her traffic with other nations. Foreigners were to be entirely debarred from the profits of the colonial trade, either import or export, and the growth and expansion of the colonies was strictly limited by this condition.

The economic policy of Colbert has impressed the minds of observers, both contemporary and in later times, perhaps more than that of any other states-man. There is indeed a tendency amongst national economists to regard him as their typical statesman,[5] and Carey, the American protectionist, called him the greatest that had ever appeared in the world. When we examine his methods we find little or nothing that was original. There was ample precedent in England and elsewhere for the main lines of his policy, but he has, at any rate, the distinction of gathering up into a coherent system and enforcing through the agents of a strongly centralized administration the leading devices that had been evolved for the establishment of a strong, self-sufficient national power.

The nature and degree of his success is in debate. His financial reforms are generally admitted to have been sound in principle and practically effective, and he undoubtedly, by his unremitting attention to industry and commerce, gave them a much-needed stimulus. But his success in this regard owed more to the character of the man than to the validity of the principles upon which he framed his policy, and we have to distinguish between the immediate and the permanent effects of the system which he established.

The favourite charge against Colbert is his neglect

of agriculture, which was involved in his concentration
on manufactures, and his check upon its development
by his restrictions not only on the export of corn but
on the internal .traffic. His policy of prohibiting
export, it is said, may have had influential justification
in famine conditions, but its continuance helped to
discourage production and so checked the development of agriculture. But in point of fact it was
Colbert's practice always to allow free trade in corn
inter-provincially ; and as to exports, he simply
pursued the old policy of allowing them or prohibiting
them according to the success or failure of the harvest,
and during the years 1669–74 an unprecedented
freedom of export obtained, Colbert apparently
basing this partly on the mercantilist reason that it
would draw the money of foreigners into the country
in payment for French grain. [6]

Colbert's system of industrial regulation, while
failing in itself to secure the ends for which it was
applied, generated a practice of evasion which hindered its application. The progress of manufactures
was by no means proportionate to the amount of
subsidies granted to them and the general effect was
to create a spirit of dependence which was fatal to
the enterprise upon which successful industry depends.
Enlightened leaders of industry indeed recognized
the defect of the Colbert system, and when asked
by him what was the best thing he could do for them
declared that it was to leave them alone. The anti-
foreign tariff led to retaliation on the part of the
English, which indeed issued for a time in complete
prohibition of French imports and helped to increase

the embitterment of the relations between the two countries which was to find expression in a second Hundred Years War. The Dutch also retaliated, and Colbert's policy must be regarded as largely responsible for the Franco-Dutch War of 1672—a war in which the French were not successful.[7]

In his colonial policy Colbert did indeed succeed in driving the Dutch from the profits of the colonial trade, but it was at the expense of great hardship to the colonies themselves, and in many respects his methods utterly failed to achieve the objects for which they were intended. In some cases indeed he himself was driven to recognize by withdrawal the ill-effects of his measures. Thus he wished to exclude Irish beef from the West Indian islands, just as the English had sought to check the import of Irish cattle into England. But the French proved quite unable to take advantage of the opening thus afforded for the shipping of French beef to the island, and the veto had to be abandoned. Again, he attempted to stop the exchange of rum and molasses for New England foodstuffs and lumber, but the trade was so profitable to both parties that the government was compelled to make definite provisions for its encouragement. This trade connexion of New England with the French West Indies was, however, viewed with such jealousy by the English Parliament that eventually, in 1733, the Molasses Act was passed, imposing heavy duties on molasses imported from foreign dominions with the exception of those of Spain and Portugal. The effect of this Act so far as it was operative was to reduce the ability of the New Englanders to take the manufactures of the home country. It was, however, to a large extent disregarded, and attempt to enforce it was one of the immediately provoking causes of the American revolt. The whole molasses question is a capital illustration of the working of French and English Mercantilism.

Our verdict on Colbert must necessarily be one of differentiation. So far as industrial regulation is concerned, immediate success was obtained only at the price of later industrial decay. The methods adopted to extend foreign trade helped to produce wars from which France came out a great loser in the end. On the other hand, his colonial policy resulted in the firm establishment of trade with the overseas dominions of the West, though at the cost of great intermediate suffering to the colonies themselves. But his success in any particular aspect of his policy must be assigned largely to the uprightness and energy of the statesman than to the soundness of the principles on which he proceeded. As Professor Marshall has pointed out, the benefits which Colbert gave to France by the protection of manufactures rather than agriculture, like those which Sully had given to France in the development of agriculture rather than manufactures, illustrate the extent to which a paternal economic system depends for its success upon the genius and wisdom of the man who dominates it rather than upon the soundness of the system itself, and Colbert, while he shared in the dominant mercantilist theory, was much more of a practical man than a doctrinaire, his prudence being shown by the way in which he would modify or abandon a line of procedure when he saw that it was obviously failing to produce the results which he desired.

Colbert's successors followed his methods without his modifying prudence, and the evils of the system were exaggerated and brought to the front by incompetent management. The financial and economic condition of France was gradually, though with alternations of revival, carried to that point of confusion and exhaustion which gave the opportunity and the stimulus for revolution. It has been suggested that if other Colberts had followed him the nation might have been led along a course of economic progress which would have prevented the rise of the spirit of revolution. But several other conditions besides the succession of Colberts would have been needed to render this a possibility, and the lesson of history is surely that a price which too often has to be paid for a Colbert is the succession of men like Colbert's successors. His policy, instead of being stayed at prudential limits, was carried to its logical extremes. Protection proceeded so far as to defeat the ends which it contemplated, and the trade that flourished was the contraband rather than the legitimate. Agriculture, industry, and commerce alike declined in the latter part of the reign of Louis XIV, though many factors besides the ill-managed mercantile system helped to produce this result. The most notable of these, the Revocation of the Edict of Nantes, which has been styled from the economic standpoint the greatest and most unpardonable folly of Louis XIV, is an illustration rather of religious bigotry than of national exclusiveness, though economic interests were concerned in its support.[8] It was as little in keeping with the Colbertism that sought to prevent other nations from profiting by the skill of French artisans as with the principles of industrial freedom, and it helped the rise of Prussia. Moreover, the rejection of the " free trade " clause in the Anglo-French treaty of 1713 came from the English side and not from the French.

During the minority of Louis XV the system of Law, whose views and measures provided a strange mixture of inflated Mercantilism and moderate free trade, gave a factitious activity to French commerce ;[9] but more useful to the general interests of the country was the pacific and economical administration of Fleury, which did much to make good the losses sustained during the War of the Spanish Succession.

In the second half of the eighteenth century the second Hundred Years War between England and France—to use Sir John Seeley's expression—passed through those stages, in the Seven Years and American Independence conflicts, which above all others were the outcome of clashing mercantilist ambitions. There can be little doubt that France, in the aid which she rendered to the American cause, was largely influenced by the mercantilist calculation that in helping to sever the political connexion between England and the colonies she would be assisting in the destruction of a source of British wealth and power which depended upon political control. There was gain and loss on both sides, but the strain was felt especially in France, where the effects of the drain of money were accentuated by the evils of mal-administration.

Nevertheless, these years witnessed the beginnings of a reaction in thought, and to some extent in practice, against the regime which on the whole had prevailed in France for more than a century, and to which students and observers naturally tended to attribute the evils from which France was suffering. Even during the reign of Louis XIV the methods and consequences of Colbertism had been severely criticized. Jurien had attacked the work of the great minister from the purely political standpoint, and de Belesbat had denounced, as responsible for the miseries of the country, the policy of trying to bring gain to France by ruining the commerce of foreigners. Boisgilbert had protested against the neglect of, and restrictions upon, agriculture.[10] The Physiocrats,[11] whose teaching gave scientific form to the French reaction against Mercantilism, confronted the Colbertist concentration upon manufactures with an emphasis on agriculture as the sole source of wealth and the Colbertist principle of industrial and commercial regulation with a general doctrine of freedom. They demanded not only a removal of all fetters upon the free circulation of agricultural products but free trade in manufactures. The attempt to secure a favourable balance of trade by means of a tariff system they condemned both as hostile to liberty and as based upon a false notion of what constituted the national wealth.

The teaching of the Physiocrats was not without effect. They had a real, if only a partial and inter-mittent, influence upon administration, and the period witnessed some slackening of the rigour of industrial regulations and some relaxation of the system of tariff protection and prohibition. The efforts of Turgot to establish financial reform and inaugurate the reign of agricultural, industrial, and commercial freedom failed before the forces of conservative prejudice and vested interests. He tried to do too much and to do it too quickly.[12] Still the new ideas made headway. Partly under Physiocratic influence, and especially under that of Adam Smith, the free trade movement was under way in England too, and the result was that after the great American war, in which England and France had been opposed to each other, Pitt was able to carry a commercial treaty with France very much on the lines of that which the Tories had been unable to carry after the War of the Spanish Succession. This arrangement has often been described as a " free trade " treaty, and its alleged disastrous effects in France have been held up as an example of the evil that may be wrought by free trade. That England gained to a far greater extent is undoubted. Pitt saw that England, whose industrial revolution was giving her great advantages in production, was so far better fitted to profit by any relaxations as to trade than was France. So indeed she was ; and this fact would in itself be sufficient to explain the large increase of English exportation to France as compared with French exportations to England which immediately followed the treaty. But to describe it as a " free trade," treaty is a misapplication of the term. The provisions bear strongly in favour of the English, and the absence of French silk goods from its application in itself robs it of any right to be called a " free trade " measure. But the opinion that the treaty, through such measure of free trade as it gave, annihilated French commerce and manufactures is not borne out by the facts. After the first sudden expansion of English exports there was a decline in these and a slight increase in French exports ; whilst as time went on the effect was to stimulate French manufacturers to imitate English manufacturers, greatly to the advantage of French industry and commerce.[18] The treaty itself is certainly open to criticism, but it had, at any rate, the advantage of bringing to an end a long war of arms and tariffs, and with revisions would have been to the benefit of England and France alike.

One circumstance which prevented France from taking full advantage of the treaty was the fact that she had not, like England, attained to that fiscal unity within her own borders which is demanded alike by Mercantilism and by free trade. It was the French Revolution which brought this boon to France by sweeping away all the tolls and duties which had hampered the transit of goods within the country itself. Industry, too, was to a large extent emancipated, privileged companies ceased to
tariff, liberal in its main basis, thou
and there with Mercantilism, was
But the Physiocratic triumph
the war went on political reasor
the old system of restriction and
especially under Napoleon with

9

ing the commerce of the great enemy—England. It seems to have been Napoleon's wider aim, in a spirit of exaggerated Colbertism, to build up a " grand industry " in France, form a strong mercantile marine, and secure for her a monopoly of the foreign and coasting trade of Europe.[14] This inflated mercantilist ambition contributed powerfully to his own downfall. But in spite of liberal opposition, the influence of vested interests and the fear of England caused the restrictive and prohibitive regime to be carried over into the years of peace.

The revived policy was maintained down to the middle of the century.[15] The adoption of free trade in England, and the rapid increase of her prosperity which followed it, made, however, a strong impression upon French opinion. Bastiat [16] was the leader of an agitation for similar reforms in France. It met with little success. The protective system was so strongly rooted that it was one of the few institutions of the ancient regime that the Revolution had not been able permanently to abolish. Louis Napoleon, however, not only recognized the success of the English reforms but believed that they might well be imitated in France, and he made considerable breaches in her prohibitive and protective policy, greatly to the advantage of French trade, before he entered into the famous treaty with England. His programme, announced early in 1860, was practically a free trade manifesto, and prepared the way for the treaty made later in the same year. On both sides the consummation of the arrangement was apparently decided by political reasons, but the economic motives must not be minimized, and there can be no question as to the beneficial consequences of the agreement. The steps towards freedom represented by this and similar arrangements with other countries [17] resulted in great industrial and commercial expansion, and the ease with which France recovered from the effects of the Franco-German War bears witness to her economic strength under the policy of the Second Empire.

France, however, had never been really converted to free trade principles, and in the late 'seventies, when, in common with other countries, and through the operations of general causes, she felt the effects of intensified competition and the almost continuous fall in prices, both agricultural and manufacturing interests clamoured for a reversal of the liberal policy which had been inaugurated by the Second Empire. Protection was demanded against the growing competition of other countries in the interests of national self-sufficiency. The campaign gradually gained its end, and the victory lay not with protection of the transitional, educational, scientific kind which had been advocated by the German List but with a protection that was typically mercantilist in its spirit and principles. In particular, the excess of imports over exports which had come about since the adoption of a more liberal policy was pointed to as a determining consideration in favour of protection, and protection was to be general for all branches of production— agricultural and industrial. The tariff of M. Méline (1892) established the fiscal system on practically its present basis. It had been preceded by a long tariff war with Italy, which injured both countries, and was followed by a brief tariff war with Switzerland, which had proportionately harmful effects. The rise of new industries and methods and the example of foreign countries led to a demand for revision, which was carried out in 1910 ; but this did not represent any real change in principle, and it may be said that in the latest age the policy of France has been generally one of national exclusiveness and self-sufficiency, based upon the stimulation, encouragement, protection, and development of home industry, the restriction of imports, and the encouragement of the exportation of surplus products by the instrumentality of bounties and tariffs.

That France has made great industrial and commercial progress during the operation of this regime is undoubted, but this has not been so striking as that which took place in the same period in free trade England or protectionist Germany and America, and has obviously been largely due to a general movement which has been felt in other countries, apart altogether from tariff policy, and perhaps connected in its cause with the enormous production of gold. Moreover, the system of bounty and protection has failed to bring any substantial prosperity to industries like shipbuilding, in which the geographical conditions of France and apparently the peculiar character of her people do not fit her to excel, whilst those trades in which the French, by reason of their artistic taste and skill, are pre-eminent, have flourished with little or no assistance from the State.[18]   Indeed, it would seem that in the more heavily subsidized industries protection has rather tended to check enterprise, and the high prices which have ruled for machinery and semi-manufactured goods have doubtless retarded industrial activity in many directions. The agricultural protection which has been the special feature of the neo-mercantilist movement in France has resulted in making her practically self-sufficing in her elementary food supply. But this has only been at the expense of her foreign trade, and, still more seriously, it has helped to restrict her population and has only been possible because of that restriction.

The World War gave a renewed vogue to mercantilist ideas and methods of State regimentation in regard to agriculture, industry, and monetary matters which had seemed to be obsolete, and one effect of the war, in France as in other countries, has been to afford a fresh stimulus to mercantilist notions of national self-sufficiency and protective self-precaution—by tariff and otherwise. But in spite of the present activity of employment there, due to abnormal conditions unrelated to her protective system, it appears to be clear that if France is to have as large a population as she may desire, the ideal of national self-sufficiency in the matter of food supply will have to be abandoned, and a system evolved whereby an increasing quantity of industrial products shall be exported to pay for the foodstuffs which France requires from abroad [19]—a development which points to a regime of freer exchange.

Whatever doubts may exist as to the character and effects of French Mercantilism so far as France herself is concerned, there can be no doubt as to the unsatisfactory results of what was long the dominant colonial

policy.[20] The old policy of exclusion was superseded at the Revolution by that of tariff assimilation,
whereby a colony was considered no longer as a domain
to be exploited but as a part of France.   This involved
a sweeping away of all tariff barriers between France
and her colonies, but as to foreign countries, the system
of exclusion remained operative.   Under the Consulate
and the Empire tariff assimilation disappeared and a
complete system of exclusion was restored, and the
same policy was maintained under the restored
monarchy.   The Second Empire, under the stimulus
of free trade ideas, abandoned the ancient colonial
system in favour of commercial freedom and tariff
autonomy, but the protective movement which
succeeded introduced a return to tariff assimilation
on a new basis, the main object of which was to make
the colonies as profitable as possible to France through
reservation of their markets for French producers.
The general principle of the assimilation was that
duties on imports from foreign countries into the
assimilated colonies should be the same as if they were
brought into France ; French merchandise was to
be admitted into the colonies duty free ; but, on the
other hand, colonial products were not freed from
duty, but simply allowed to come in at a considerably
reduced rate.   This policy of colonial subordination
produced much discontent in the colonies affected,
on the ground that it involved the sacrifice of their
interests to the supposed, though not the real, interests
of the mother country.   Hence arose a movement
for revision which resulted in 1912 in the exemption
of colonial products, with certain exceptions, from all

customs duties in France. The more advanced colonial reformers, however, demand not simply reform but the adoption of a new principle—tariff personality, involving, as they urge, the recognition that the real interest of France lies in the prosperity of her colonies.

CHAPTER IX

HISTORY OF EUROPEAN MERCANTILISM
—GERMANY

IN considering the history of Mercantilism in England, France, and Spain, we have been concerned with political entities representing united nations, and with the application of expedients consciously designed to increase the national power. Germany, on the other hand, from the later Middle Ages down to the later nineteenth century did not possess any really effective central authority, and the State or semi-State policies which we encounter within the limits of the German land during the greater part of that period are mostly those of territorial princes, often warring amongst themselves, or taking different sides in European conflicts, aiming, so far as they attempted any definite economic regime at all, at a self-containedness which was provincial rather than national, and having little regard to any ideal of German unity. Yet during these centuries, vexed with war and internal strife, the broad tendency of thought and of political action was slowly making a path for the movement of unification which was to result in 1870 in the establishment of the federal German Empire.

The stages in the history of German Mercantilism are closely bound up with the successive phases of the

political evolution of Germany. The exclusive
economies of the towns set the example for the Mercantilism of the territorial princes, which found its
supreme embodiment in the industrial and commercial
systems of the founders of the modern Prussian power ;
and there is no great difference in fundamental spirit
between the Mercantilism of Frederic the Great and
the neo-Mercantilism which in the latest age has
characterized the policy of the German Empire under
the presidency of his descendants. Moreover, the
teaching of the Cameralists, who were the German
Mercantilists—though also something more—of
the seventeenth and eighteenth centuries, contained most of the elements of the social economy
of the nineteenth- and twentieth-century German
State.

At the close of the Middle Ages, that is, about the
end of the fifteenth century, German industry and
trade were flourishing, but anything in the nature of a
national organization of economic life and activities
did not exist. So far as the idea of German unity
had any concrete expression, this was to be found in
the imperial office and organization, but the authority
of these had greatly declined as the result of causes
with which we have not here to do. The Holy Roman
Emperor, who claimed to be something far more than
a king of Germany, was in reality far less, and the
entanglement of Germany and Italy with the formal
representatives of western Christendom, the Empire
and the Papacy, only helped to hinder each of them
from attaining the unity of a national State. In
contrast with England and France, where Tudor and

Valois were building up strong national monarchies, Germany was divided, so far as political and practical control is concerned, amongst a multitude of territorial princes, lay or ecclesiastical, whose lands were seldom geographically contiguous, nobles, knights, and imperial cities.   Industrial activity was centred chiefly in the towns, which maintained themselves as independent exclusive economic units, concerned only for the interests of their own citizens and residents, and defended themselves by taxes, tolls, and restrictions from the encroachments and competition of other towns and their inhabitants, though sometimes, as notably in the case of the Hansa League, common interests in external trade drew them together in a federal union.   In conflict with these independent town economies was the attempt of the territorial princes to extend their power over all the area within which their possessions lay, and establish therein a territorial economy which should regulate town and village economies alike ; but this process had as yet made little headway.   It was, however, in accordance with the tendency which contemporaneously prevailed in other countries towards the control of the economic life of the people by the prince.[1]

As previously remarked, the teaching of the humanists, who harked back to pagan ideals, favoured the increase of the power of the prince on paternal lines.   The *Institute of a Christian Prince*, by Erasmus, which was dedicated to the Emperor Charles V, was essentially of this character, and some of his counsel, as when he advises that a sovereign who is in need of supplies should levy them on the goods of foreign merchants, is eminently mercantilist in spirit. It is said that this recommendation had some influence in producing a scheme which if it had been carried would have been a definite step towards the welding together of the German peoples. It was proposed in 1522, in order to provide for the maintenance of the imperial chamber and government and the general expenses of administration, to raise a toll along the whole imperial frontier on the whole foreign trade of Germany. The object of this proposal, as indicated, was primarily fiscal, but it fell in with an opinion which obtained widely amongst the non-mercantile classes that the country was a loser by the money which went to pay for imports, and that the tax would operate as a check upon this loss, though it failed to satisfy the logical corollary that the export trade was correspondingly gainful, for it was to be levied on imports and exports alike. The scheme, however, was vigorously opposed by the towns, whose representatives urged that a tax of this sort would utterly ruin German industry and commerce and lead to the emigration of artisans and mercantile people to foreign lands. In view of the multitude of custom houses already in existence, they did not desire to see a fresh series along the whole frontier of the Empire. The other estates retorted that the proposed tax would not affect necessaries of life. Other nations had imposed similar taxes for the common good without ruining trade and commerce, and in any case the profit of a few tradespeople must not be rated above the common welfare, which would undoubtedly be subserved by the way in which the money would be spent. The opposition of the towns, however, prevailed. It has been denounced as anti-national and purely self-interested, as thwarting a zeal for union proceeding by way of tariff reform. But it is to be noted that the feeling of the towns, apart from the financial aspect of the matter, was directed not so much against the idea of German unity as against the aims of the princes, who, as they conceived, sought to use the imperial machinery rather for their own than for the common ends.[2]

The Reformation helped to confirm the movement towards princely independence. The leading German reformers, wishing to win the support of the secular arm in the various parts of Germany, tended to emphasize the power of the prince, and their teaching, in its general purport, favoured a sort of territorial Mercantilism in which all departments of the social and economic life of a people should be under the paternal control of the prince. It thus also encouraged the movement in the direction of territorial sovereignty. In the financial and economic sphere this movement found expression in an assertion, in which Hapsburg Austria and Hohenzollern Brandenburg led the way, of absolute independence of the empire and of other princes in the matter of taxation, and an extension of princely control at the expense of the town economies. There was nothing of national spirit in all this. Rather we are called upon to witness, during the sixteenth and seventeenth centuries, what has been described, from the German standpoint, as a civil war of all against all,[3] in which one territory set up tariff obstructions against another territory, and territorial and town economies fought for the mastery, greatly to the detriment of German industry and trade.

Then came the Thirty Years War, during which Germany was the unfortunate battle-ground of both German and foreign rivalries and ambitions, and which completed the ruin that had begun in the period of reform.[4] The imperial power survived, but was reduced almost to a nullity. Industry and commerce had fled to less troubled lands, and a sadly depleted population was left in a country which had been largely laid waste by war. But from the standpoint of mercantilist history the main result that stands out at the peace of 1648 is the triumph of the principle of territorial sovereignty. The territorial princes obtained the confirmation of all their rights and pretensions, and it was to them that fell the task of directing the revival of national life. They were definitely secured in various regalian rights, including those of levying taxes, coining money, maintaining an army, and even that of concluding treaties with foreign powers provided that these were not directed against the Emperor or the Empire. The possession of these rights and the impoverished condition of the people opened the way for the conversion of territorial rule into princely despotism, and most of the princes, being devoid of any broad national aim, were not loath to seize the opportunity.

The most obvious political phenomenon of the age was the gorgeous power of France, and it was the effort of the German princes to imitate, within the narrow limits of their petty States, the absolutism of Louis XIV and the Mercantilism of a Colbert. The policies of the territorial princes in their practice and their ideals were partly reflected in, and partly stimulated by, the teaching of the Cameralists, some of whom were themselves engaged in the work of administration.[5] Cameralism has been labelled as German Mercantilism, and for its beginnings we have to go back to the teachings of the reformers in its bearings on princely economy, but it was not till after the Thirty Years War that its systematic presentation really commences, when Seckendorff, who has been well described as the Adam Smith of Cameralism, produced in *The German Princely State* (1655) the first treatise in German on the subject. Other writers followed, and almost a century later Cameralist doctrines and practices were gathered together and systematically summed up in the work of Justi. The object of Cameralism was the power and welfare of the State, which they regarded as the source of all other welfare. They assumed an absolute power in the ruler, and the royal income, its maintenance, increase, and administration, was the central subject of their inquiries—as was indeed not unnatural after the financial exhaustion caused by the Thirty Years War. Economic subjects and policy thus formed a leading part of the content of their science, and both the spirit in which they approached these subjects and the methods which they advocated in relation to them corresponded very closely, like the spirit and methods of the rulers whom they served, with the teaching of the mercantilists. They had similar views in regard to government regulation, the precious metals, population, national self-containedness and international competition. But being mainly concerned with land powers they devoted less attention to foreign trade and the " balance " idea than did English and French mercantilists, and they made more of agriculture than Colbert had done. They were mercantilists, but also much more. Their subject was political science, and covered a variety of legal, political, administrative and technical matters with which Mercantilism in its narrower sense had no concern. Their works, which are but a systematization and idealization of the policy which was being developed in the German States of their time, contained in embryo, it has been said, everything which is distinctively characteristic of the German social polity familiar to our own times. That policy was pursued with varying degrees of intelligence and consistency in different German States, which came to present during the eighteenth century almost every kind of quasi-absolute administration, from that of a petty narrow bureaucracy to the large and efficient despotism of the house of Brandenburg-Prussia.

Nowhere else in Germany were the principles of a territorial Mercantilism carried out with anything approaching the energy and resoluteness displayed by the rulers who, during the latter half of the seventeenth and the greater part of the eighteenth centuries, were engaged in establishing that Prussian power which, during the next century, after the fall of the Holy

Roman Empire and after the ousting of Austria from the headship of Germany, was to stand forth as leader of a German Empire which should represent a real and effective German unity. Indeed, the stretch of years from the accession of the Great Elector in 1740 to the death of Frederic the Great in 1786 provides, in the history of Brandenburg-Prussia, a unique example of the rigorous and consistent application by successive rulers of mercantilist doctrines and expedients to the building up of a strong and self-sufficient State.[6] It is unnecessary to enter into any lengthy account of the system. It was practically the system of Colbert pursued to even greater lengths, extended to agriculture as well as manufactures, but minus the maritime, colonial, and extra-European aspects of his policy. In order to recruit the population and revive cultivation and industry after the Thirty Years War, emigrants from other countries, particularly Holland and France, and especially those who could bring with them knowledge of, and skill in, useful arts, were encouraged. The absorption of Protestants from France was the beginning of a period of renewed prosperity for Brandenburg-Prussia. What were considered to be necessary industries were established, supported, and subsidized by the State, controlled by minute regulations, and protected from the competition of foreign imports by actual prohibitions or prohibitory duties, and the diplomacy of the State was also employed to assist manufacturers in the disposal of their products. In the interests of manufacturers, the exportation of raw material was forbidden. Frederic the Great, be it added, paid special attention to the development of agriculture. Whilst on the one hand he introduced the rearing of silkworms, and planted thousands of mulberry trees, he propagated, against an active resistance, the culture of the potato, which he regarded as an admirable resource for the poor.

The greatness of the work of Frederic the Great is undoubted, though the figures which are often quoted to illustrate it are apparently misleading, and give an exaggerated impression of the economic progress made by Prussia under her mercantilist rulers.[7] There was, indeed, progress, but it was slow. It was attended with innumerable inconveniences, and there were radical defects in the system which were bound to show themselves when the hand of the great master was removed. A few years after his death there was published in London an elaborate work written in French, in which the Prussian monarchy under Frederic the Great was subjected to a critical examination.[8] The treatise appeared in the name of Count Mirabeau, though Mauvillon, son of a Frenchman who had settled in Germany, was the substantial author. Writing under the influence of the Physiocrats and Adam Smith, who is described as a " man of genius " whose work, *The Wealth of Nations*, already become " in some sort a classic," is " a monument that can never perish," the authors set forth the principle that government should confine itself to matters of defence, the administration of justice, and the maintenance of order, and leave to industry the greatest possible liberty. They point out the falsity of that balance-of-trade theory which was a leading

10

principle in mercantilist policy, and proceed to show the soundness of the free trade ideas by examining the condition of that country—Prussia—which had been subjected to a more rigorous system of protective regulations than had been known in any other land, applied by the genius and resources of "the most wonderful man who has ever carried a sceptre." Their conclusion is that though there had been an increase of commerce in certain directions, this was by no means due to the prohibitive system. It was only part of a general increase in Europe, and it was doubtful whether in point of fact Prussia had obtained a proportionate share of the expansion. Except in cloth and rural products, Prussian commerce was indeed languishing. The profits derived from the regime were problematical; the inconveniences were undoubted, and a system of agriculture, industry, and commerce, which depended not upon natural development but upon State initiative, subsidy, support, and relief, could not be regarded as in anything but an unhealthy and precarious condition.

While the authors of this work perhaps unduly reduce the measure of the royal achievement, they at any rate hint at its main defect in dependence upon the continuance of a strong administration consistently applying the principles, however mistaken, to which it was committed. The weakness of the regime became clear after the death of Frederic, when the succession of outstanding rulers came to an end, just as the defects of Colbert's system became visible after his departure. Such a system indeed demanded a succession of directing genius and energy of which there can never be any assurance. Under weaker kings and ministers, and in the midst of new political and international complications, Prussia suffered the ill-consequences of the extraordinary concentration of affairs which it had required the extraordinary genius and energy of Frederic the Great to maintain; and the Napoleonic epoch reduced her to utter confusion.

This, however, was the beginning of a rise to greater power. The circumstances of the time provided a favourable hearing for the anti-mercantilist teaching of the Physiocrats and Adam Smith, for which Mirabeau and Mauvillon had pleaded, and the influence of those views, the application of which was, according to them, to " save the world " and " restore the human species," is seen to some extent in the measures whereby Stein and Hardenberg helped to save and restore the Prussian State.

In his considered statement of what in his view was needed for the welfare of Prussia, Stein set forth a doctrine of free industry and trade in language which might well have been inspired by that of *The Wealth of Nations*, and though his actual policy fell far short of the fullness of freedom, the programme of reforms which was carried through by Stein, Hardenberg, and other ministers of this epoch mark a sweeping departure from the eighteenth-century mercantilist regime.[9] The emancipation of the peasants and the establishment of free trade in land were in the nature of a social revolution. The State ceased to concern itself directly in the promotion of industry by bounties and other financial assistance. Prohibitions of imports were removed, and high duties made low. There can be no doubt that this policy of economic liberation contributed largely to the rise of Prussia out of the political humiliation and internal confusion into which she had fallen, and when, in 1818, the whole of the tariffs which had long obstructed traffic amongst the numerous territorial fragments of the kingdom were swept away, and the fiscal unity of Prussia was established on the basis of internal free trade, a step was taken which though not consciously so intended was the beginning of a movement in the economic sphere which, along with progress in other departments, was ultimately to issue in the unification of Germany under the presidency of the power which had led the way towards fiscal unity.[10]

The fiscal union of Prussia was followed, under the stress of practical necessity, by its extension to adjacent German States. Similar unions were formed in other parts of Germany, and the movement reached its climax in the formation of the Zollverein, which by the middle of the nineteenth century included practically the whole of Germany with the exception of Austria. Thus Prussia obtained and Germany obtained that boon of internal free trade which England had long enjoyed, and which in France was one of the most important permanent achievements of the Revolution.

But though the German fiscal unions, minor and major, were based on the principle of internal free trade, their policy in its external reference was one of moderate protection. The period during which the movement was in course of development was marked by a definite reaction against the vogue of what was called " Smithianismus " in Germany. Müller and List, the pioneers of this reaction, met the individualism, on the one hand, and what they held to be the unduly cosmopolitan trend, on the other, of Adam Smith's teaching with a doctrine of National Economy. Müller [11] in particular stressed, the virtues of the State and State regulation, the permanent claims of national interests and power, and the normality of international strife, in a spirit which was fundamentally reactionary and mercantilist. List,[12] though preaching the doctrine of National Economy with far more eloquence and vigour, made more concessions in theory to the ideals of the classical economists. Cosmopolitanism and universal free trade were lauded by him as ideals, but, he held, economic policies must have regard to, and be determined by, the particular stage of development at which a country stood or had arrived, and not by the assumption of ideal conditions which did not in fact exist. In his emphasis on the relativity of economic policy to the conditions of time, places, and people, List ranks as a pioneer of the historical school, though his reading of history is coloured and disturbed by that nationalist sentiment which was the main stimulus of his thought and action. The real world, he observed, was organized in separate nations, which were in constant strife and competition with one another, and the people that desired to maintain itself and flourish could only do so if it followed the principles of national power. Universal free trade was the ideal which might one day be realized, but in the meanwhile a free trade system was only safe and wise for a country that had attained a high degree of industrial and commercial advancement. England, for instance, had reached such a position, and could well afford to practise free trade ; but a country where manufactures were but in the nascent stage could not stand without State protection against nations that were more advanced. List, indeed, did not hesitate to represent the English free traders as advocating free trade for less developed industrial nations out of national self-interest, as it would make such nations less able to resist the aggressive enterprise of English traders. Whilst List strongly advocated an " educational tariff " for nascent industries, he condemned, and advocated the removal of, such assistance when a country's industrial and commercial development was matured. Yet, with all his allowance for the free trade ideal, the main stress of his argument, especially for Germany, was on the cult of national strength by a vigorous policy of protectionism for manufactures, though not for agriculture. He criticized with much shrewdness not only the teaching of the Physiocrats and Adam Smith but that of the Mercantilists.[13] He condemns the latter for the rigid and indiscriminating character of its system of prohibition and protection, and its failure, in the exclusive pursuit of the political object, to allow for the principle of cosmopolitanism, and to recognize that the future union of all nations, the establishment of perpetual peace, and of universal freedom of trade was the goal towards which all nations have to strive, and more and more approach. But his main polemic is directed against the school of the classical free trade economists, and his main admiration is reserved for national mercantilist policy whereby, as he conceived, England had established her industrial supremacy, for the mercantilist regime which Colbert had imposed in France, and for the mercantilist system which for more than a century the Hohenzollerns had practised in Brandenburg-Prussia, and his leading theme was that on the development of the German protective system depended the existence, the independence and the future of the German nationality.[14]

The teaching of List to some extent may have influenced, and at any rate fell in with, a tendency towards increased protection in the German tariffs, but, in defiance of the specific argument with which he had supported his thesis, the expansion of English prosperity after the definite adoption of the principle of free importations helped to stimulate a movement in favour of imitating not the past but the present commercial policy of that formidable power, especially after the negotiation of the commercial treaty between England and France, and the 'sixties and early 'seventies show a deliberate movement in Germany in the direction of free trade.

The year 1870 saw the culmination of that movement towards the unity of Germany under the presidency of Prussia, which had really started with the abolition of the Holy Roman Empire in 1806 and the revival of Prussia which began shortly afterwards. Her inauguration and control of the movement for fiscal union had enabled her in time to oust Austria from that leadership of Germany which had still been left to her after the great French war. It is worthy of note that the maintenance of a policy of comparative free trade in the Zollverein was one of the means adopted by Prussia to keep Austria, whose tariff system was strongly protective, out of the union.

The foundation of the German Empire, which marked the triumph of nationality in Germany as it had previously triumphed in Greece, Belgium, and Italy, was not followed by any immediate disturbance of the free trade policy in favour of a regime of national protection. The prosperity which had attended its adoption gave no temptation for change. The extraordinary activity which was produced by the influx of the French indemnity, however, was followed by a reaction and a period of depression and low prices which had no connexion with fiscal policy but was due partly to the special circumstances of Germany after the war and partly to general causes, especially the improvement in the means of transport which brought a new and active competition from the West that affected all the countries of Europe. These conditions gave new life to the protectionist movement in Germany as well as in other countries, and in 1879 Bismarck, who had hitherto ranked as a free trader, became a convert, practically, if not theoretically, to the policy of national protection. The establishment of the policy was greatly assisted by English dumping in the German market and by the beginning of the conversion of the landowners to the idea of protection for agriculture in consequence of the competition from Russia which the opening up of the railway system had brought upon them. There has been much discussion as to Bismarck's motives, but it seems clear that he was influenced partly by the idea of the protection of national industry and agriculture and partly by considerations of finance. He wanted money for the imperial exchequer. Indirect taxation would be less unpopular than direct. Hence an increase of customs dues seemed to be the only way. Industry and agriculture needed protection, and this could only be effected by an increase of customs dues. Hence he aimed at a system of duties which should be sufficiently high to be really protective, but not so high as to stop imports altogether and so produce no revenue at all. Whatever the relative weight of financial needs, industrial protection, and agricultural protection in his thoughts, Bismarck inaugurated that policy of protective tariffs which remained the normal policy of the German Empire, accentuated with the increase of tariffs in other countries, and modified by commercial treaties.

For a time the accent was rather on industrial protection, but the rapid growth of an increasingly industrial population led to an agrarian movement which had for its object to put a check to the conversion of Germany into a mainly industrial State. The national self-sufficiency which was aimed at was impossible without an adequate food supply, and the strength of the nation, it was urged, really rested on a numerous and healthy agricultural population. The protection of the agricultural interest should therefore be the first aim of national policy, and all other interests should be subordinated to it. Partly under the influence of this teaching and perhaps particularly out of a feeling of the importance of ensuring an adequate food supply in time of war, the emphasis of protectionism in Germany was transferred, in the later stages of the empire, to the side of agriculture, and the tariff on manufactures was low as compared with that of other leading protectionist powers.

In regard to industrial and agricultural products alike, the influences of the relevant interests have conspired to maintain the protective system, and when one argument, like that of " infant industries " has become obviously out of place, another has been found to justify the continuance of the regime. But while the force of private interests has affected the details of German protectionism, the leading features of Germany's economic policy have depended upon far more general considerations. Doctrines of free trade and *laissez faire* have never taken deep root in Germany. The creation of the empire in 1870 was the most conspicuous triumph of the nationalist movement of the nineteenth century, and with the foundation of a strong imperial government the way was prepared for the development of a neo-Mercantilism in which the paternalism that was the persistent tradition of the German States should be applied to the regulation and regimentation of industry and commerce in the interests of German self-sufficiency and power on a scale commensurate with the authority of the new political union.[16] The revival of protectionism, largely mercantilist in temper, which under the stimulus of the new vogue of the idea of nationality and the new conditions of international competition took place in other countries, helped to bring out and accentuate the tendency which was really implicit in the movement of German unification as related to German history and tradition. The tariff was employed by Germany, as by other representatives of the neo-mercantilist movement, as a weapon of political and economic protection and aggression, but in the sphere of industry at any rate Germany trusted less to the tariff than did other protectionist countries, and the wall which she built up against, say, English manufactures, was considerably lower than that maintained by France, far lower than the barrier erected by the United States, and low indeed when compared with the Russian scale.

The speciality of German neo-Mercantilism has rather consisted in the resolution with which she adopted and applied other methods of national consolidation and advancement, her State regimentation of education and industry at home, and her policy of expansion and penetration abroad.[16] In face of the cult of exclusiveness and self-sufficiency pursued by other protectionist countries, where the pressure on the national resources has been much less urgent, Germany, with the limitations imposed by nature upon her internal possibilities, and the rapid growth of her population, addressed herself increasingly to a far-reaching policy whereby she might secure control, preferably political, of those additional markets and resources which were, as she considered, essential to satisfy the clamant and prospective needs of the

German people. This combination of political and economic aims and ends is, as we have seen, of the very essence of Mercantilism.

It is a commonplace to remark that the industrial progress of Germany has been one of the most striking phenomena of the latest age, but its causes are too complex to be reduced to a simple statement. The view that attributes it largely to the abandonment of a free trade policy by Bismarck in 1879 is too superficial to demand explicit confutation. Whatever may have been the precise effects of the tariff, the advance of German industry and power has been the resultant of a combination of factors, amongst which, if the tariff has its place, it is but a subordinate place. Far more significant has been that capacity for the organized application of science to industry and for sustained teamwork, which has been the characteristic contribution of Germany to the necessities of large-scale production.[17] Moreover, in some respects it is clear that the protective system in Germany has hindered healthy development,[18] favouring some classes, agrarian, industrial, and social, at the expense of others, buttressing low prices in the foreign market with high prices in the domestic market, and if it cannot be held altogether responsible for the low rate of German wages, it at any rate failed to raise them to a level at all corresponding with the position of Germany as an industrial nation.[19] In the wider sphere, whilst the revival of protectionism generally has tended to the embitterment of international feeling, the methods adopted by German neo-Mercantilism in its efforts after political and economic expansion served to produce for her that isolation amongst the nations which rendered ultimately futile the war insurance which had been a leading aim of her system, and helped to bring upon her the final disaster.

CHAPTER X

HISTORY OF MERCANTILISM—AUSTRIA, ITALY, SCANDINAVIAN COUNTRIES, RUSSIA, JAPAN

NEARLY all the States of Europe shared more or less in the historical mercantilist movement, and though most of them participated in the supervening tendency towards a more liberal system, which was partly confirmed and partly induced by England's successful adoption of free trade, the great majority joined sooner or later in a protectionist revival which has not yet been exhausted. It is not possible in this chapter to do more than briefly summarize the courses of development, whether typical or exceptional, in some of the European countries that have not so far been noticed, in the Euro-Asiatic empire of Russia, and in her Asiatic island neighbour, Japan.

The economic regime of Austria received a strong mercantilist impulse while the house of Hapsburg still normally enjoyed the elective headship of the Holy Roman Empire, and Joseph II, in his active industrial and commercial policy, was not the least arresting of the mercantilist reforming monarchs of the eighteenth century.[1] In this aspect he may be compared with Peter the Great of Russia, Frederic the Great of Prussia, and Charles III of Spain. The mercantilist spirit persisted, though with no real national basis in the heterogeneous Hapsburg dominions, after the abolition of the Holy Roman Empire, when Austria, after an interval, was left with the presidency of the loose Germanic confederation. As we have seen, Prussia used a comparatively low tariff in the Zollverein as a means to keep protectionist Austria out of the union, and afterwards managed to drive her out of the German system altogether. The Austrian regime was considerably modified during the period of liberalized tariffs in Europe, but Austria entered early and fully into the succeeding protectionist reaction. The development of her alliance with the Hohenzollern German Empire is a subject that cannot be treated here, but more significant for her fortunes than her own protective policy was her subservience, in recent years, to the mittel-Europa scheme whereby German neo-Mercantilism sought to obtain, for political and economic reasons, an effective control over the region from the North Sea to the Persian Gulf. This subordination helped to bring Austria into the greatest of wars, and thus to precipitate the break-up of her empire.[2]

Just as a preliminary step to the unification of Germany under the Hohenzollern was the extrusion of Austria from the German State system, so the unification of Italy required the expulsion of Austria from Italy, and this was accomplished by the aid of the power which ousted Austria from Germany. Under the guidance of Cavour, Piedmont had adopted a liberal commercial system. His economic ideas were largely formed in England, under the influence of the classical economists.[8]　He believed that England had prospered in the past not on account of protection but in spite of it and had prospered most where there had been least protection, and part of his policy of making Piedmont a model State which should win the respect of Europe and the confidence of Italians all over the peninsula was to frame her economy on the free trade lines with which England had replaced the Mercantile System.　With the union of Italy all local tariffs were abolished, and the comparatively liberal scale of Piedmont became the national one.　Later, however, Italy fell in with the current reaction against economic liberalism.　One of the consequences was a long tariff war with France which seriously affected the trade between the two countries.　It is indeed difficult to see what benefit Italy derived from her protective system, which seems to have rather checked than assisted her economic progress, and the settlement of her quarrel with France and a modification of her tariff led to a definite improvement in her industrial and commercial position.　Jealousy of French colonial adventures had caused Italy to combine with Germany and Austria in a Triple Alliance.　Feeling against Austria rooted in questions of national frontiers led Italy to enter the Great War against Austria.　Since the close of that conflict she has joined in the outburst of apprehensive national protectionism by raising her tariff rates to about double what they were before the war.　But it would seem that in so doing she has studied rather immediate security than future progress and expansion.

In all the Scandinavian countries a rigorous Mercantile System prevailed during the later seventeenth and the eighteenth centuries.[4]   Denmark, in particular was greatly hampered by her prohibitive and protective regime, which involved an artificial development of manufactures for which she was not fitted, at the expense of agriculture and commerce.   Partly because of the concrete evil effects of the regime and partly under the influence of Physiocratic teaching, she definitely abandoned it towards the close of the eighteenth century, and inaugurated a liberal commercial policy which has been more or less consistently maintained since then.   In recent decades Danish agriculture, which is concerned mainly with stock-raising and animal products, has flourished exceedingly on the basis not of protection but of co-operation, though the government assists it by supporting societies and institutions devoted to its improvement. Schleswig, since her withdrawal from the German protective system, under which her agriculture had been languishing, is beginning to share in Danish agricultural activity.   Danish manufactures, too, have prospered without tariff protection.   Indeed, few countries supply in their history so marked an illustration of the burdens of the old Mercantile System, and the possibilities of progress under a free trade regime accompanied by well-organized industry and enterprise.

The economic policy of Sweden and Norway during the last hundred years have proceeded upon different lines from those on which that of Denmark has moved. Norway, formerly linked politically with Denmark became politically associated with Sweden in 1815, each preserving its independent economic system. Both countries retained a mixture of prohibition and protection in their regimes, both of them subsequently shared in the " free trade " movement, and both of them joined in the protectionist revival. But Sweden both lagged behind Norway in the liberal movement and, influenced by depression of trade and the example of other countries, returned much sooner to a protectionist regime, with the cry " Sweden for the Swedes." An unfavourable " balance of trade " played a prominent and perhaps determining part in causing the return of Norway to protection. Since the dissolution of the dual monarchy the spirit of nationalism has been much intensified in both countries, and has strongly influenced their economic policy. The neo-mercantilist movement in Sweden and Norway has been especially evident in measures to bring the water-power in which these countries abound more under State or native control, in the attempt to protect and conserve the iron ore deposits in the national interest, and in the assistance of shipping by subsidies and in other ways. The policy has not passed without domestic criticism on the ground of its possible effects upon economic relations with other countries, particularly owing to the attitude towards foreign capital which it involves, but as yet it would seem to be too early to pronounce upon its results.

The history of Russia has a threefold significance in connexion with our subject.[5] In the early eighteenth century she was the scene of one of the most thorough applications of mercantilist principles

that have ever been attempted. During the neo-
mercantilist movement of the later nineteenth century,
Russia led the way in high tariff protection ; and in
recent years she has carried out a drastic political
and social revolution, the excesses of which are largely
to be explained by those of the previous paternal and
despotic regime, in its mercantilist as in its other
aspects.

Though the first of the Tsars, Ivan the Terrible,
endeavoured to develop commercial relations with
England, Holland, France, and other countries to the
west, Russia may be said to have belonged to Asia
rather than to Europe until the closing years of the
seventeenth century, when Peter the Great commenced the task of introducing into his empire the
conditions and factors which, as he believed, were
responsible for western progress.[6] He hoped thereby
to lay the foundations, if not to complete the structure,
of a self-sufficient national State. Peter took extraordinary pains to qualify himself for his chosen work.
He travelled in many western lands with a view of
obtaining not only by inquiry and observation but
through the actual labour of his hands a clear insight
into, and understanding of, their industrial and commercial systems. Peter was especially impressed with
what he learnt and found in England and Holland,
and fully absorbed the prevalent mercantilist ideas.
Not content with his own observations alone, he sent
Saltykov to France, England, and Holland, to study
the operation of their economic regimes. Soltykov,
in his report, dwelt particularly upon the English
policy and practice, and urged, in the light of them,

that national manufactures should be created, so that Russia should no longer be tributary to the foreigner ; that commerce should be developed so as to secure a favourable balance of trade, for which purpose the establishment of privileged companies and financial support to them would be necessary ; and that manufacturing industry should be supplemented by a well-organized rural economy—an essential condition of national self-sufficiency. The Baron de Luberas also submitted to the Tsar his views on the proper economy of the Russian Empire. Its prosperity, he held, would depend upon due attention to two things— navigation and industry. Sharing the common opinion of the time, de Luberas noted that England had arrived at a flourishing condition under the rigorous regime of Cromwell—the navigation system by which, as he mistakenly thought, all merchandise shipped from or to England was carried exclusively in English vessels. Holland also, he added, sought profit from navigation so as to attain a favourable balance of trade, and the Scandinavian countries were attending to it. De Luberas set before Peter the prospect of Russian predominance in commerce, and the Tsar's own supremacy as the benefactor not of Russia only but of all the world.

Drawing upon his own experience, and making use of ideas thrown out by others, Peter the Great was pre-eminently a convinced mercantilist reformer, deter-mined to give to his country, and do for it, what he held to be good and necessary, in spite of all obstacles that lay in his path. Proceeding at first empirically and later by systematic plan, he employed nearly all the expedients that western mercantilists had applied, and likewise other devices, with a degree of State domination surpassing, within the area of its effectiveness, anything to be met with in the States of western Europe. Foreign artisans were brought over to teach their trade to the natives. New industries, like those of silk and woollen, were founded. Convicts and idle persons were forced into the industrial army, and a new class of serfs was thus created. On the one hand, home industry was assisted by prohibitions and protective tariffs, whilst on the other it had to submit to minute regulations as to the form, quality, quantity and price of its products. Ships were built and companies for foreign trade were started. Peter also attempted to promote a vigorous rural economy, but on the whole agriculture was treated as subsidiary to manufacture, and was comparatively neglected.

The economic life of Russia received a great stimulus from the efforts of Peter the Great, but the reforms that he effected were to a large extent artificial, and not lasting. They constituted rather an imposition upon, than an education of, the people. He introduced industries that were hardly appropriate to the character of his subjects, or the stage of development at which they had arrived, and the products were unsatisfactory both in quantity and in quality, whilst his commercial companies achieved little. Moreover, the serfdom on which his system was based bore heavily upon the people.

Peter the Great stamped upon the Russian national economy the notes of prohibition and protection, government supervision and control, which have characterized it, with modifications, down to our own time.[7] It is needless to trace its development with any particularity, but some of its main phases must be indicated. The influence of Adam Smith, which was communicated to the official classes in Russia chiefly by von Storch,[8] an adherent, though not a blind one, of the teaching of *The Wealth of Nations*, caused or assisted a trend of opinion in favour of a more liberal economy in the years succeeding the peace of 1815. The doctrine of non-interference found some favour, and changes were made in the tariff in a free trade direction. But this movement was very short-lived. The ideas of regulation and control were too firmly implanted in the Tsarist and official mind to be more than temporarily disturbed. A return to protection took place in 1822, and Russia has never since then enjoyed a really liberal commercial system.

During the vogue of relative free trade on the Continent, due mainly to England's example, the Russian tariff was lowered—though remaining on the whole decidedly protective—in order to secure the admission of Russian agricultural produce and raw materials to the markets of western Europe; and the free importation of railway iron at this time rendered possible the construction of the network of lines which have been justly described as by far the greatest cause of the development of Russian industry. Moreover, in this period occurred the emancipation of the serfs, which was of high moment for the future of Russian history.

In the late 'seventies, however, after the concessions

had served their purpose, the tariff was restored to practically its old basis, and the appearance of Russia as an agricultural competitor in the west in the " free trade " period and her subsequent reversion to high protection were important factors in stimulating the neo-mercantilist movement in Europe generally.   The full development of Russian tariff protection came in 1891, when it led to a customs war with Germany. Apart from the tariff, the Tsarist State assisted industrial undertakers both financially and by land, mine, and timber concessions, and the spirit of a paternal government was exhibited in a system of minute supervision and regulation.   Home industries increased to meet the requirements of the domestic markets, but the expansion of commerce was restricted by the customs wall, and although the amount of industrial products came to exceed that of agricultural products, the bulk of the people were still engaged in agricultural pursuits.   Such prosperity as Russia enjoyed during the last generation of Tsardom was based rather upon her natural riches than upon her protective regime, which indeed bore oppressively upon the people.   The subsidies and tariff support that manufacturers obtained from the government so kept up prices that many Russian products cost more in Russia than they did abroad, and wages were miserably low.   As the system was in the interest of a class rather than of the people generally, and was worked by a corrupt and incompetent bureaucracy, it undoubtedly helped in producing revolutionaries.

The defeat of Russia in the Japanese war furnished the revolutionary movement with its first great opportunity, and within a decade the situation created by the World War brought about the complete overthrow of the old order in Russia.   The fall of Tsardom, the trial and failure of republican absolutism, the violence and confusion of the Soviet regime are, however, topics too large for discussion here, and it remains to be seen how far the spirit of dictation and restriction which, with difference of detail, informs the new as it did the old regime will give place to the principle of political and economic liberalism on which depends the peace of the world.

Whilst some significant distinctions may be drawn between the protectionism of the countries so far considered and the Mercantilism of earlier times, the Far East supplies in Japan the example of a State which during the latter part of the nineteenth and the earlier part of the twentieth century has exhibited allthe essential conditions, accompanied by most of the characteristic expedients, of historical Mercantilism.

The opening up of the country to foreign trade about the middle of the last century marks the entrance of Japan into the complex of international economic relations.   The merging of the feudal units into the comprehensive unit of the State in the early years of the reform era laid the foundations of the central authority which was essential to the establishment of a national system of economics ; and the rulers of Japan addressed themselves in an eminently paternal spirit to the consolidation and expansion of the national power by the vigorous cultivation of the country's economic resources on the lines which had been familiar to the west in the system practised particularly by Burleigh in Elizabethan England, and by Colbert in France. In the extent to which it has involved the copying and introduction of foreign ideas and methods it reminds us especially of the work of another great mercantilist, Peter the Great, in Russia.[9] All the old-time expedients of the system —bounties, subsidies, exemptions, privileges, and a protective tariff—have been applied by Japan to the development of her industry, commerce, and marine. Her general aim has been to discourage imports except of such goods as were unprocurable within the country, and to encourage exports so as to increase national production, establish a favourable balance of trade, and render the nation economically self-sufficing and independent. The part played by the conception of the balance in Japanese policy is understandable in view of the fact that with her entrance into foreign trade it was necessary to build up a financial reserve. Hence the efforts to establish the currency on a gold basis —an end which has been pursued by the regulation of the tariff so as to secure an influx of gold, and by the exercise of control over the export of gold.

The industrial progress of Japan during the present century has become a commonplace of observation, but it required conditions altogether unconnected with her fiscal policy—the unprecedented circumstances of the Great War—to bring about her greatly desired favourable balance of trade. Up to the time of the war, in spite of her tariff, the value of imports had almost always exceeded that of her exports. But now Japan, though a belligerent, was, unlike the other allies, able to pursue her industries in the ordinary course, and the heavy demand upon her for goods, supplies, and shipping services gave her the desired surplus of export values, caused a growth of her mercantile marine second only to that of the United States, and enabled her to register a continued increase of her gold reserves. It is indeed doubted whether previously the policy of subsidizing exports did not serve to thwart the purpose of a favourable balance of export values inasmuch as it tended to keep the values low in spite of an increase in volume, whilst rebates and subsidies in shipping helped largely to nullify that redress of the balance which might otherwise have been afforded by the earnings of the Japanese marine.

But with all the temporary prosperity the economic situation of Japan has presented many illustrations of the inconveniences attaching to a mercantilist regime. In pursuing the aim of diversification of industry she has given the aid of the State to industries for which she is not specially fitted and which even with artificial aid can hardly compete at profitable rates in the markets of the world, instead of allowing a natural concentration upon manufactures for which she has natural facilities. Moreover, only in a very partial and limited sense can Japan be said to possess the conditions of economic independence. In the event of isolation her food resources would be barely self-sufficing, and the industries which are necessary to her prosperity are, except so far as silk is concerned, mainly dependent upon raw materials from abroad. Some of the efforts that have been made to remove this dependence have, as in the case of wool, been costly failures. Again, the vogue of State aid has had a demoralizing effect in that it has generated a habit of constantly looking to government assistance for any business or industrial adventure.[10]

The collapse of the boom and the sending back of the trade balance, however, brought Japan into the wave of the post-war protectionist revival. But the difficulties and discontents in which she found herself were hardly to be cured by an intensification of the regime that had helped to cause them. With the continued increase of an already immense population the ruling out of a mercantilist policy of territorial expansion pointed the way rather to a solution of the problem of development and maintenance in the evolution of a freer trade system whereby Japan should pay by her manufactures for the raw materials and food stuffs she required. The catastrophe of the earthquake has but sharpened the stress on the claims of ultimate interdependence

CHAPTER XI

HISTORY OF AMERICAN MERCANTILISM

ENGLAND, in her maintenance of free trade, has stood in contrast to most of the leading nations of Europe. She has stood in still more marked contrast to the countries of the New World, and it is a notable fact that her past and present colonies in that region have been amongst the leading representatives of the protectionist movement. It may indeed be said that American protectionism grew, as it were, out of the soil of English Mercantilism.

Though the American colonies may have suffered little under the old colonial system, it is still fair to describe their rising as a revolt against that system. Its articles were not—could not be—consistently enforced, they were easily evaded, England gained little from her possession of the colonies, whilst it would seem that their industrial development proceeded on very much the same lines as they would have done if they had enjoyed economic independence. But it was the belief on all hands that colonies, duly subordinated, were a source of wealth and strength to the colonizing power. The American colonies had been able to appeal to this mercantilist sentiment in England in asking for protection against the encroachment of the French at the time of the Seven Years War. The relief which they secured as the result of that war largely helped to produce the spirit of independence. They now resented the idea of colonial subordination which was expressed in the system, but in accordance with the tenets of Mercantilism they believed themselves invaluable to England, and after the failure of their attempts to break down the system by their own devices, they made skilful use of the idea of their value to England in appealing for the assistance of powers that envied the strength which England was supposed to derive from her colonies. The liberation of the American trade for their benefit was a strong inducement to their support of the American cause. But the result of the war proved the falsity of the basis on which the Americans had proceeded in this connexion. It did not alter the natural commercial relations of England and America, and the fact that England, though she had lost her political control over the colonies, was able to do an increasing trade with them, did much, as we have seen, to discredit the old mercantile colonial system, and to give a vogue to the teachings of the Physiocrats and Adam Smith.

Mercantilist regulations, however, and the mercantilist temper, still prevailed in the industrial and commercial policies of Europe, and it is hardly surprising that during the struggle of the Americans with the Mercantilism of the Old World, the mercantilist idea of national economic independence should have found expression amongst them, and that, in Alexander Hamilton, the new nation should have produced the pioneer advocate of that policy of national protectionism which, while differing from the old Mercantilism in some detail and degree, is yet its derivative and its representative.[1]

It has been said that the system of protection presented in Hamilton's famous *Report on Manufactures*, is the old system of Mercantilism turned round and adjusted to the situation of the United States.[2] In point of fact, Hamilton's views mark a definite advance on the old Mercantilism. He sees the final advantages of free trade, and regrets the excess of the mercantilist restrictions. Yet, in their dominant spirit, and in what may be called the immediacy of their application, his views are essentially of the mercantilist order. The influence of Adam Smith is seen in his argument against the Physiocrats as to the sterility of manufactures, but he was the first essentially, if not consciously, of the nationalist critics of *The Wealth of Nations*. His aim was primarily political. He sought the establishment of the effective unity of the United States to enable her to hold her own against the established nations of Europe. To this end, economic independence was essential. Hence he preached the promotion of manufactures so as to make America self-sufficing not only in respect of agriculture but in regard to industrial products, and he urged the protection of such manufactures by tariffs, bounties, and the like, during the period of their infancy or establishment. The lack of skill and experience which in Hamilton's view made such protection necessary in the United States was attributed by him largely to the repressive policy of the British in regard to colonial manufactures. Hamilton had the true mercantilist belief in the value

of State direction and regulation, though perhaps
not to mercantilist extremes. He also set forth the
preservation of a favourable balance of trade as a
leading motive of policy, though here again he seems
to have had some notion of the limitation of the
logical implications of this principle.

Hamilton's teaching had little effect for the time
being, though a growing feeling for protection was
reflected in the American tariffs.[3] The prosperity
which the United States enjoyed during the earlier
phases of the great French war helped to postpone the
triumph of the movement, but in the later stages,
during the operation of the Continental System and
the Orders in Council and the Anglo-American hostilities arising out of them, the United States was thrown
back upon herself. Her manufacturers enjoyed for
the home market an actual protection such as they
had never before experienced, and new industries were
created to meet the call. The peace necessarily
involved the removal of the war restrictions upon
imports. The consequent inrush of foreign goods,
especially English, created amongst the manufacturing
interests an alarm which generated a demand for some
such protection by means of a tariff as had been
afforded by war conditions. The teaching of Hamilton
to the effect that every nation ought to endeavour to
possess within itself all the essentials of national
supply—means of subsistence, habitation, and defence
—was again brought forward, and secured presidential
adoption. 1815 saw, in the passing of the Corn Laws,
the last positive enactment of the English Mercantile
System. 1816 saw the first definitive protective

American tariff—the beginning of that American policy which in its larger, continental reference, was to find expression in the Monroe doctrine. This early protectionist movement reached its culmination in the Tariff of Abominations (1828), which may have owed something to the influence of List, who was in America at that time, as well as that of the writings of Hamilton. It certainly was influenced by contemporary American conditions. In view of the important part which the "infant industries" or "educational tariff" has played in protectionist propaganda it is worthy of note that one of the most judicial students of American tariff history, writing with special reference to the legislation of this period, arrives at the conclusion that although there then existed in America the conditions under which it is most likely that protection to young industries may be advantageously applied, yet little or nothing was gained by the protection which the United States maintained in the first part of the nineteenth century.[4]

The system, which was supported by arguments of a distinctly mercantilist tone and temper, was vigorously resented by the Southern States, who did not share in the manufacturing interests of the north, and contended that taxes were placed mainly on things which were used by them and expended for the benefit of other parts of the country. It was pictured by Southerners as comparing unfavourably even with the old mercantile colonial system of England. The restrictions imposed by the tariff States upon the commerce of the planting States were, declared one Southern representative,[5] a hundred times more injurious and oppressive than all the restrictions and taxes which Great Britain had imposed or attempted to impose upon the commerce of the colonies. "A revolution which severed a mighty empire into fragments originated in restrictions and impositions not a whit more tyrannical in spirit and not a hundredth part so oppressive in point of fact as the restrictions now imposed upon the Southern States. The prohibition which excluded our ancestors from the commerce of all other countries but Great Britain was almost purely nominal. Without that prohibition, the trade of the colonies would have been confined almost exclusively to the mother country. The Southern States are to all intents and purposes re-colonized, as much as if the British Parliament had the supreme legislative power of regulating their commerce." Whatever may be thought as to the truth of the picture thus presented, these expressions are interesting both for the view of the old colonial policy which they set forth, and because the tariff question was one of the contributory elements in the quarrel which ultimately burst out into Civil War.

The extreme protectionism of 1828 was relaxed a few years later, but the tariff wall remained high till about 1846, when, partly by way of natural reaction and partly under the influence of the English free trade movement, a modification was effected, and down to the eve of the Civil War what has been called "a free trade regime" prevailed in the United States, though in point of fact it can only be so described in comparison with the preceding rigour of the protective system.

12

During this phase of American tariff policy the advocates of protection were by no means silent, and the main work of the most ardent of all American protectionists, Carey,[6] belongs to these years. Carey started as a free trader, but ended as an advocate of absolute protection, and was by far the most popular and voluminous champion of nationalist protectionism. The work in which he summed up his main teaching appeared at the moment when the " free trade " movement in the United States had reached the farthest point to which it was destined to go, and can hardly have been without influence upon the reaction which was soon to follow. Carey attacked the free trade policy of England as making her more and more dependent upon the rest of the world—a policy which was sure to lead to disaster —and urged for his country a policy of national protection and self-sufficiency. His arguments are ingenious and original, but so far as they are new they are more specious than sound, and in their bearing upon practical policy they amount to little more in some respects than the older Mercantilism. Carey lays an exaggerated stress on the amount of money or the precious metals in a country, and presses for the maintenance of an overbalance of exports as compared with imports, as the only means to secure the necessary surplus of money. He denounces the " free trade " policy in America at that time as tending to create ar unfavourable balance, and so impoverishing anc weakening the country.

When the Civil War broke out, the trend toward a protective reaction had already begun, but it wa the situation then created by the financial necessities of the country that brought about the establishment of a protective system which was to become the firmly established policy of the Union. The requirements of the war caused the imposition of heavy taxes, not only internal but external, and as a relief to the pressure of the internal taxation the manufacturing interests demanded—and obtained—the enactment of heavily protective duties upon their products. The protective regime thus established in war survived when the war was over, and was the real basis of the American tariff till recent times. It was not in its origin the result of a deliberate protective policy, but it created vested interests which opposed any withdrawal of the protection they had received, and where industries had been established on the faith of the tariff it was urged with much plausibility that a return to free trade or relative free trade would mean their ruin. The internal taxes disappeared, but the protective duties, which had originated as an offset to these, remained. There can be no doubt, however, that, apart from private vested interests, the revival and firm establishment of protectionism was partly due to a strengthened feeling of national exclusiveness which was itself a product of the war and its result in the maintenance of the Union, just as later the unification of Germany as a result of the Franco-Prussian war opened the way for the neo-mercantilist movement in that country.

As time went on the " infant industries " argument was of necessity abandoned, and the idea of national self-sufficiency, based especially upon the preservation of the home market, assumed increasing prominence. The " pauper labour " contention, which pleaded the necessity of protection to prevent the depression of American high wages owing to the competition of ill-paid European labour, also figured freely in protectionist propaganda. The tariff became not only the centre round which private and corporate interests waged conflict but the leading topic of controversy between political parties. The McKinley tariff of 1888 was marked especially by the protection which it gave to agriculture, and the Dingley tariff of 1897, which remained in operation till 1913, brought American protection to a climax.

During the regime of high protection America rose to the position of the greatest industrial nation in the world, and the advocates of protection have not unnaturally seen in this fact an illustration of cause and effect. But a sober consideration of American history leads us to the conclusion that the tariff has played a far less important part in the progress of American industry than might be imagined from the extent to which it has figured in political controversy.[1] There had, in fact, been a proportionately rapid development in the period of relative free trade, and in view of the natural advantages possessed by the United States, and the alertness and enterprise of her people, it seems clear that her industrial advancement would have been equally marked with a tariff for revenue alone. Apart from the tariff, America has been comparatively free from the mercantilist regulations, and it has been upon the freer elements in her industrial and commercial system that her prosperity has mainly rested—especially upon the possession of an enormous home market with free trade within the whole of its area. Indeed the success which has attended the establishment of manufactures in the more backward parts of that area, with no protection against the more advanced industrial regions, afforded striking testimony to the ability of infant industries to flourish without artificial assistance.

With the illusion that the protective tariff has been the main factor in the development of American industrial greatness is the connected opinion that it is responsible for the high standard of wages enjoyed by the American workman. That it may cause wages to be high in a particular industry at a particular time is undoubted, but a consideration of the various elements affecting wages makes it clear that the general high level of American wages has depended not upon tariff protection but upon the productivity of American labour. In point of fact, while wages have been high in America under protection they have been low in Germany, and the degree to which they have increased in Germany has been due not to increased protection but to an increase in the productivity of German labour, and Germany became a more formidable competitor with this increase of productivity and wages. The plea for protection, as a safeguard for home wages against the " pauper labour " of other countries, which has bulked largely in American protectionist arguments, seems to be based upon a false conception of the influences that determine wages.

The more sinister effects of the protectionist system

are much more easily traceable than the good. On its influence in the corruption of political life it is unnecessary to dwell. The growth of trusts in its more malignant aspects appears to have depended largely upon the protective tariff, and if a high tariff has not been responsible for high wages, it has certainly been a main factor in high prices, so that if we examine the history of wages and prices during the period of high protection in America we shall find the increase in real wages less in the United States than in England.

In the years before the war, however, there were signs that the protectionist movement in America had spent much of its strength. It began to be seen even amongst protected manufacturers that the high costs of production, which were largely due to the tariff, were handicapping them in the markets of the world, and the increased cost of living and the unwholesome power of the trusts became connected in the popular mind with the high protectionism under which they were apparent. Hence a reaction in favour of a modification of the Dingley scale which after a revision in 1909 found expression four years later in the most striking reversal of American tariff policy that had taken place since the establishment of high protection about fifty years before, and ordered a scale of duties which was on the whole more moderate than anything since the days of relative free trade.

The advent of the Great War prevented this reform from exercising what would have been its effect in normal conditions, and the economic results of the upheaval for the United States depended very little upon the state of the tariff. The main general effect from our present standpoint is that the part which America played as the great supplier of the needs of Europe converted her from a "debtor" to a "creditor" nation. The so-called favourable balance of trade, consisting of an excess of exports over imports, which America, according to the mercantilist or protectionist view, enjoyed before the war represented not a gain by her to the extent of the difference in value over other nations but simply the payment through exports of the interest on foreign loans and investments in America, and the freight on the services of foreign shipping and other dues. She now became, however, undoubtedly a creditor nation, the greatest in the world, and it was not obvious how her debtors could make any present progress in the liquidation of their debts to her except by way of goods, just as previously she had paid her debts in exports. But the collapse of the foreign demand, with the beginning and prospective increase of an influx of foreign products, provoked a new protectionist movement. Whatever might happen in regard to the debt to America, it was urged, home industries must be protected from this competition, and the domestic markets preserved for them. Increase in importations must be checked to prevent the favourable balance of trade from turning into an unfavourable one.

A policy of protection, it was contended by one of its advocates, was simply nationalism translated into terms of economic science, and the national interests required it now. "It appeals to the sentiments of patriots, to the logic of human events, and the necessities of life. It is a broad and national application of a great principle laid down in the Mayflower Compact, the Declaration of Independence, the Federal Constitution and the Monroe doctrine."[8]

Against this mercantilist view of national independence, the American free traders have contended that it was a mistake to prevent debtors from paying in the only way in which they were able to pay. Imports must of necessity increase till they surpassed exports, and the crude mercantilist notion of the balance of trade based on the opinion " What I gain you lose " must give way to a recognition of the mutual advantages of the exchange of goods and services. America could not permanently remain an isolated, self-sufficient nation. She had already reached the stage when she was barely self-feeding. As time went on she was bound to become increasingly industrialized, and to depend more and more upon foreign demand for her manufactured products. A condition was developing which was fairly comparable with that of England from the close of the eighteenth to the middle of the nineteenth century, when she ceased to be a food exporting and became a food-importing country with a rapidly growing export of manufactures, and when ultimately manufacturers themselves came to ask for a reduction of tariffs and removal of other mercantilist restrictions.

To that last stage, however, America has not yet attained, and the new and greatly heightened tarif registers the triumph for the time being of the pro tectionist reaction.

In another direction, however, a movement for th

re-establishment of mercantilist regulation has so far not been brought to a definite conclusion. A subject of great concern for American statesmanship is the future of the mercantile marine. The earlier policy of the Republic, following upon the lines of the English Navigation Acts, was to protect American shipping as a national industry by means of discriminating duties. But after a time this was succeeded by a policy of reciprocity, and gradually by mutual treaties the special protection of American shipping was abandoned. The industry flourished until the supersession of wood ships by iron and other improvements in construction robbed America of the natural advantages which she had enjoyed in the matter. The failure of the United States to build up a strong mercantile marine under the new conditions has been the subject of much discussion and controversy. It has obviously been largely due to the protective policy which was for long pursued in regard to shipbuilding material and American labour, and recognition of this fact led to some modification of the restrictions, but the protectionists have put it down mainly to the policy of subsidy and bounty adopted by other countries, and the absence of any special protection on the part of America. Hence the introduction of material subsidies, though with little effect, and the inclusion in the Underwood Tariff Act of a provision for a discount of five per cent on all duties in the case of goods imported in vessels registered in the United States. This, however, was not to affect the provisions of any treaties between the United States and other countries, and as practically all the countries whose shipping might be affected had treaties providing that there should be no discrimination against their goods or shipping the clause was of no practical force.   But the Great War gave a strong stimulus to the movement for the creation of a powerful mercantile marine, both on economic grounds and as a naval auxiliary. With the entrance of America into the war there began an activity in shipbuilding which made the United States the possessor of a quarter of the world's tonnage, able to carry over sixty per cent of her foreign commerce, and with a determination to maintain shipbuilding as a permanent national industry, and a merchant marine as a national asset, even at some economic sacrifice.   In this connexion the allowance of Adam Smith in regard to the Navigation Acts that though economically mistaken they had a political justification on the ground that " defence is more than opulence," was cited, and a definite policy for the protection of American shipping on mercantilist lines was inaugurated.   The Merchant Marine Act passed in 1920, which was the first substantial expression of this mercantilist reaction in regard to American shipping, includes a clause providing that all articles in treaties restricting the right of the United States to impose discriminating duties on imports or tonnage dues shall be terminated, and the President was instructed to serve notice of this abrogation.   The effect of this would be to bring into operation that provision in the Underwood Tariff Act which granted a five per cent reduction in the duties on all commodities imported in American ships, thus returning to the use of the mercantilist weapon whereby the young Republic had sought to fight the Mercantilism of the Old World. President Wilson refused to carry out the instruction, and though it was supposed that his successor would fall in with the requirement, the idea of denunciation has apparently been abandoned. The problem presented by a multitude of unemployed ships remains, and preferential measures are being discussed,[9] but there are not wanting those who denounced the mercantilist reaction on the ground that discriminations invariably lead to international ill-will and retaliation, and in the long run are ineffective as aids to national shipping.[10]

There is an obvious parallel between the courses of events in connexion with the old English-American and the old Spanish-American empire. Both insurrections were more or less revolts against the Mercantile System, and it is not without significance that the new nations of the south who had won their emancipation from Spain formed their constitutions on that of the United States. At the same time the differences are not less marked.[11] The life of the North American colonies of England had been far less restricted than that of the Latin American countries under Spain. They were therefore prepared for liberty. But the old colonies of Spain were not equally fitted for their new-found freedom. The mere imitation of the formal characteristics of the United States constitution was therefore not sufficient to enable the Latin American republics to pursue a progressive constitutional course. The effects of a long subordination upon the character of the people could not be done away with in a moment or even in a generation. Though the colonies had thrown off the yoke of Spain and Portugal, they became bound in practice to a system of control both in the political and in the economic sphere. Politically, the United States has been able to assert a protectorate over the whole of the American continent south of its own territory under the principle of the Monroe doctrine, whilst economically the fact that industrial developments in Latin America have been carried out mainly with the aid of European money has naturally subordinated economic life there to the control of European capitalists, though in the latest age the commercial interest of the United States in Latin America has been increasing. The republics have built up high tariffs which are usually regarded as eminently protective in character, and they undoubtedly contain protective elements, but it would seem that on the whole they are based upon revenue considerations arising out of the special conditions of industry, commerce, and social life in the countries concerned.[18]

CHAPTER XII

HISTORY OF MERCANTILISM IN THE BRITISH DOMINIONS AND IN INDIA

THE fiscal policy of the British colonies that have attained self-government has taken a very different line from that maintained by Great Britain herself. In each of the dominions, partly from general, partly from special causes, a protectionist regime has become established. India, moreover, under her new constitution, has started tentatively, and the trend of her nationalist feeling favours a systematic movement, upon the same path.

Canada obtained fiscal autonomy during the period when Great Britain was step by step making her tariff a free trade one, but as time went on, she employed this liberty in setting up not free trade but a system of national protection which had much in common with the mercantilist regime that the mother country had abandoned; and which was much influenced in its development by the example of the United States.[1] The policy that was evolved aimed at national isolation and exclusiveness, at securing the home market for Canadian productions, and making Canada independent of all other countries, and its advocates invariably pointed to the industrial progress of the United States as evidence of the fruits of protection. They called for a defensive tariff against American and British competition alike. " Canada for the Canadians ! " was the cry.

The year 1879, in which Bismarck became a practical convert to protection, also saw the definite legislative inauguration of the national policy for Canada in the form of a tariff aiming primarily at the protection of home industries. It was especially directed against British imports. The large extension of the dominion borders that had taken place since the establishment of the federal constitution had doubtless something to do with the intensifying of the national idea. From this time there was built up in Canada a protective system which though not so marked as that of the United States in the height of the tariff wall, has presented more of the mercantilist element in the way of bounties, and other aids to industry, and in government supervision generally. In its emphasis on the " national " idea, on the paternal regulation and encouragement of industry, and on the balance of trade—which has at various times exercised an important influence upon Canadian tariff movements —the policy of the dominion has exhibited leading features of the Mercantile System.

It cannot be said that the " national " policy of Canada has achieved its objects, even if we give to the " national " ideals a somewhat reduced interpretation. With the firm hold of protection in the political system, manufacturers have been able to secure the imposition of increased duties even when trade has been so prosperous as to furnish no support for the concession, and the reliance upon high protection thus engendered has tended to demoralize the industries concerned. At the same time, whilst consumers have been taxed in high prices, the tariff has proved only partially successful in giving the protection that it has been intended and supposed to afford. The extent to which it has served the revenue has often been cited as a sign of flourishing conditions, but this has been clearly indicative of its relative failure to prevent the import of competing goods.

A modification of the national policy was introduced when a preference was granted to Great Britain, but this change did not mean an abandonment of protection against British goods ; it only effected a discrimination in degree, and at any rate in the early stages of preference the combines that had grown up under the protectionist system were able so to manipulate prices that consumers failed to get the relief they had expected. The post-war period has witnessed some reduction in the tariff and in turn a demand for increased protection of home industries. As, in spite of preference, imports from Great Britain have been decreasing, whilst purchases from the United States have been increasing, a feeling of alarm at the growing " economic dependence " upon the United States has arisen, with a call for measures to diminish it. The revived protectionist campaign, however, has met with considerable strength of opposition, owing largely to a revolt amongst the farmers against a regime which seems to sacrifice the interests of agriculture to those of industry.

Before Great Britain turned to free trade, the Australian colonies, like the American, were subject to the regulations of the Mercantile System. It was

thought that after the adoption of the new policy by
the mother country, the colonies, as they gained fiscal
independence, would use it in harmony with the more
liberal economic ideas now in vogue. But this expec-
tation was disappointed, and the record of the tariff
relations of the colonies for many years is a somewhat
unedifying chapter in Australian history.[2] Protection
found its great protagonist in David Syme,[3] of Victoria, where the movement was much influenced by
the "infant industries" argument, which by many
free traders has been made a guarded exception to
their condemnation of protection, and later, as in the
United States and Canada, by the "pauper labour"
theory, whilst Liberalism in Victoria was driven into
association with protectionism largely through undue
interference or attempted interference by the mother
country in the affairs of the colony. New South Wales,
on the other hand, stood almost consistently for free
trade, and at the time of confederation she enjoyed
far more prosperity than did protectionist Victoria.
Yet, when the Commonwealth was founded, though
it swept away the tariff barriers that had hindered commerce within the limits of the Australian continent,
and thus created a large free trade area, the voice of
Victoria was sufficiently powerful to secure the enactment of a protectionist tariff against the outside world,
though the scale adopted was much lower than that
which had prevailed in Victoria. The tariff has been
modified in relation to the mother country by the
grant of a substantial preference, but the minimum
duties have been left at such a height as to afford what
is conceived to be sufficient protection to the "infant

industries " of Australia. There, as in other lands, the post-war years have witnessed a revived protectionist movement which has resulted in the raising of the tariff wall.

The mercantilist aspect of Australian policy has been illustrated in forms of State regulation besides that of protective duties, and a notable feature has been the support of protection by the Labour party, with the condition that the benefit derived by manufacturers from the tariff shall be reflected in rates of wages and conditions of labour.[4] But whatever the effect may have been as to the home market, the protective regime has seriously limited the possibilities of progress in markets abroad. The experiment of subsidies has been of little avail in this direction, and the reconciliation of the claims and interests of internal and external trade presents a difficult problem for Australian statesmen under the existing system.

Upon the fiscal policy of the other dominions it is unnecessary here to dwell. Suffice it to say that both New Zealand and South Africa practise protection with preference. Concerning the imperial preference controversy something will be said in the closing chapter.

Not only does protection obtain in the dominions, but, as already observed, the nationalist movement in India has a definitely protectionist bias. Historical and contemporary conditions alike have contributed to produce this characteristic.

The Indian nationalist tends to look upon the British governance in India as one which has involved the economic subordination of his country, and some

13

idea of the interpretation of history that is brought to the support of a policy of national protection there may be gained from an essay by one of its advocates. During the greater part of the East India Company's rule, contends this writer,[5] India was treated on the one hand as a source of raw materials for British industries and on the other as a compulsory market for British industrial products. British goods were admitted into India at merely nominal duties, whereas Indian goods had to pay heavy duties within the country, whilst their entry into Great Britain was either absolutely prohibited, or practically prohibited by the height of the tariff wall. Thus the inland trade was discouraged, and India's foreign commerce directed for the benefit of Great Britain, and native industries previously flourishing were destroyed. When Great Britain went over to free exchange, the new regime was extended to India without regard to the wishes of the people—indeed in opposition to them, and she was not allowed to develop any industrial enterprise if it happened to come into competition, even in a remote or indirect manner, with any British industry.

This version of Anglo-Indian economic relations overlooks various elements in their historical make-up, and there is " another side " which is not stated, but its representation of the Mercantile System as applied to India is only what might be expected, and in the later period, so far as freedom of imports was accompanied by a practice or policy of repressing domestic manufactures, there was obviously a failure to satisfy the requirements of all-round freedom of trade.

Reaction against the past and consideration of the examples of the British Dominions, the United States, Germany and, perhaps particularly, the oriental example of Japan combined in producing amongst the natives a feeling in favour of national protection,[6] the use of the tariff as " a weapon of defence, if not also of offence, in the industrial struggle," and in its more moderate form the movement won English sympathizers. It has greatly increased in strength since the Great War, and a few customs duties of a protective kind had already been imposed, before and since the setting up of the new constitution, when the Government of India appointed a mixed commission to go into the whole question. Its report, issued in 1922,[7] was definitely in favour of moderate protection. It urged the need of industrial development in India and held that without the stimulus of protective duties the advance would not be sufficiently rapid. It considered, however, that indiscriminate protection would entail a sacrifice on the part of the consumer out of proportion to the beneficial results, and it recommended that the " infant industries " selected for protection should be such as ultimately would well be able to stand alone. The question of preference was discussed with reserve, but the principle was laid down that no preference should be given to Great Britain that would diminish the protection given to native industries. The minority report, signed by most of the native members of the commission, was less moderate, and indeed favoured an " intense policy of industrialization " under the shelter of protective duties.

There is nothing new in the arguments advanced in the commission's report. The " infant industries " plea reminds us that industries protected on this ground have a way of never growing up to a sufficient extent to cease to need, or at any rate receive, protection ; and there is the usual mixture of protectionist and revenue considerations. Already, however, steps have been taken in the direction of duties imposed primarily for the protection of what are regarded as essential industries. The wisdom of the new departure is open to serious question. To say nothing of the feeling of perturbation which was created in Lancashire by the import duty laid upon cotton piece goods, there are many in India who are strongly opposed to a tariff policy which, as they hold, can only benefit home, at the expense of foreign, trade and only protect manufacturing interests at the expense of the mass of the people.

CHAPTER XIII

MERCANTILISM, OLD AND NEW

OUR survey has made it abundantly clear that the general trend of economic policy in the modern age has been determined mainly by mercantilist considerations. This historical feature is beyond controversy, and it has been held that, however strongly we may criticize or condemn the system in theory, mercantilist methods have been dictated to the nations of the world by the very circumstances in which they have found themselves in the course of their development and their contact and conflict with one another—that, indeed, the Mercantile System, forced upon the nations by necessity, has been the leading factor in their economic upbuilding and advancement. All that we can necessarily infer, however, from the historical vogue of Mercantilism is that it has usually been the economic first thought of self-conscious nationalism, and has tended to be its last thought too. Exceedingly diverse have been the fortunes of the nations that have practised the common national policy, and the question of its practical wisdom, effects and meaning is one which has to be decided upon the accumulated evidence in regard to particular na
nations in groups or in general.

It is by way of a more connected examination of

the later phases of the movement that we shall be best led to a general conclusion of the matter.

The Mercantile System has often been noticed as a regime which was developed and established amongst the growing nations of the modern world and which flourished until the late eighteenth century, when certain changes in economic conditions and the thoughts of men led to its decline and fall. But, in point of fact, Mercantilism, though it has had its ebbs and flows, has never been a spent force. It is true that the expansion of credit and banking, the Industrial Revolution, and the teaching of the Physiocrats and Adam Smith caused a movement towards freer commerce, that the pronouncements of the Congress of Vienna upon the slave trade, the navigation of rivers, and the rights of aliens, seemed to indicate that the powers of Europe, however limited their conceptions in some respects, were in others out-growing the narrowness of Mercantilism,[1] and that the example of England in throwing the system overboard assisted and stimulated a liberalizing tendency in the commercial regimes of other countries. But these effects were only partial and temporary. Of all the great States, England alone has turned her back, and kept it turned, upon the Mercantilist doctrine for any lengthy period, and in the form of protectionism a new Mercantilism became established in most States in the latter part of the nineteenth century. We have already remarked that this nation and that entered into the movement, but have said little as to its general causes and aspects, and these may be considered briefly now.[2]

There came about a natural reaction against the extreme doctrine of *laissez-faire*, and a conviction revived that far more functions were properly assignable to the State than what were allowed to it under that teaching. In England itself, even during the period in which she was changing over from protection to free trade, the force of interventionist ideas in regard to conditions of labour was sufficient to procure the passing of the first general Factory Act. The Industrial Revolution, which converted England to free trade, was attended in England and in other countries with excesses, abuses, and distresses that provoked the rise of a movement for the transformation of social conditions, a movement which in what may be described as its constitutional form looked to securing its end by means of legislative measures. The spread of socialistic ideas amongst the new industrial classes undoubtedly assisted the cause of State intervention in industry and commerce. Socialism and neo-Mercantilism, with all their dissimilarities, were alike in being reactions against *laissez-faire* and in the spirit of protectionism as to the interests with which they were primarily concerned.[3] The neo-Mercantilism of Bismarck illustrates his sense of the parallel in its combination of a policy of national protection with one of State Socialism. The appeal made to the workers by the " pauper labour " argument in the United States, Canada, and Australia, and the support of protection on terms by the Labour parties in the dominions, furnish a definite point of contact between the two sets of interests.[4] Emphasis on the State as power reached its highest pitch in Germany; the idea of State authority has had a strong hold in France; and in other countries the tendency has been generally towards increased government activity.

Along with the reaction against *laissez-faire*, the ventures of the spirit of nationality, stimulated by the French Revolution and the Napoleonic attacks upon the European system, which found their most striking triumphs in the establishment of the kingdoms of Belgium, Greece, and Italy, the preservation of the American Commonwealth from disruption, the foundation of the German Empire, and the dissolution of the dual monarchy of Norway-Sweden, contributed to the formation or re-formation of a policy of national protection alike in the more and the less democratic States. The present protectionist system of the United States was practically founded, as we have seen, during the war for the preservation of the union, and in Europe the new German Empire became the leading representative of neo-Mercantilism.

Rapid industrial progress and the enormous development in the means of communication and transport, bringing the various parts of the world more closely together, as it were, gave stimulus and character to the movement. Thus steamships and railways enabled America and Russia to send their products increasingly to western Europe and it was in the conditions of intensified international competition thus produced that the mercantilist revival became pronounced, with the increased employment of the tariff as a weapon of defence and offence in the strife.

Again, the ancient expedients of the European nations made their appeal to the national spirit of the awakened East, as we have seen in Japan, and those colonies of England which had advanced to self-government turned, in evolving their economic policies, rather to the methods by which, as they conceived, England established her industrial greatness than to those which she employed in her supremacy. Thus a national protectionist policy was definitely inaugurated simultaneously in Canada and the German Empire. Eventually the note of protection became the common characteristic, with variations, of the fiscal regimes of political entities old and new, alike in the eastern hemisphere and in the west.

The protectionist regime was really only a resumption, with adaptations, of the old Mercantile System. Under it, prohibitions have rarely been imposed, except in time of war, and the scale of duties has generally not been so high, though there has been a large range in this matter. For the employment of mercantilist expedients new reasons have been given, in addition to, or in place of, the old. It has been neo-Mercantilism, but Mercantilism all the same.

The common aim has been national economic self-sufficiency. Under the industrial conditions of the latest age, that has really been an impossible ideal for any of the nations of Europe operating solely within their own continental borders. Hence arose a scramble for territory or spheres of influence in other lands, with the object of securing or controlling their resources of raw material and the services of

their people for the colonizing, conquering, or dominating power. This movement has been styled the
expansion of Europe.[5] The acquisition of territory
or political control in southern America with its vast
and tempting riches was barred by the Monroe doctrine
—which did not, however, save Mexico from partial
absorption by the United States herself—and the
interest of Europeans there has been confined to its
economic development with their capital. The expansion therefore proceeded in parts of Africa, Asia, and
the Pacific, and the scramble was mainly in Africa.
The interconnexion of this colonial enterprise, the
ranging of the European powers amongst themselves,
and the employment of mercantilist expedients is
strikingly evidenced in the relations of France and
Italy. Thus the French occupation of Tunis was
much resented by Italy, who had hoped for a protectorate there, and this feeling on her part enabled
Germany to draw her into a Triple Alliance with
Germany and Austria. The entrance of Italy into
this grouping was in turn resented by France, and so
in large measure helped to lead on to an injurious
tariff war, lasting practically ten years, between
France and Italy. Just as the new protectionist movement, apart from general causes, was in some sort
an assertive reaction against the industrial and commercial supremacy of Great Britain, so, apart from
general causes, the development of colonial enterprise amongst the European powers was in some
measure an assertive reaction against the wide extension of the British Empire. Yet Great Britain joined
in the scramble, largely, it would seem, out of appre-

hension that if she did not enter into it she might find herself excluded by protectionist powers from markets that at present were open to her. In former times she had won lands overseas and endeavoured to reserve the advantages of commerce with them to herself. But now, in accordance with her new economic policy, whilst securing additional territories, markets, and resources, she did not, on the whole, seek to prevent other nations from sharing in their benefits. Whilst those of her colonies which had advanced to the acquirement of self-government mostly followed the leading nations of Europe in establishing protective systems, Great Britain not only maintained a free trade policy at home, but preserved the same principle in all her dependent colonies. The protectionist nations have usually assimilated the tariffs in their colonies to their own, retaining a preference for the mother country, though it should be observed that Germany did not introduce tariff discrimination in her colonies.[6] England stood out against the leading industrial nations in both west and east, and against her own self-governing dominions, as a completely free trade power wherever she had the controlling voice.

This conspicuous distinction generated a tendency in some quarters to explain a change which took place during the latter part of the nineteenth century in the relative economic positions of England and other countries by reference to their respective fiscal policies. The most obvious phenomenon in this connexion was the rapid industrial progress of Germany and the United States, and the loss by England to the United

States of her pride of place as the chief industrial nation of the world. The essential argument of the Tariff Reform movement, which, inaugurated under the banner of Imperialism by Mr. Chamberlain after the close of the South African War, gathered within its ranks all the forces of protectionism which had been pursuing an ineffective campaign ever since the revival of protectionism on the Continent in the late 'seventies, was that England was suffering from the effects of " one-sided free trade." [7] The hope of Cobden, it was said, had been that all the other countries would be stirred to follow England's example. If they had done so, all would have been well. But they had not done so for more than a limited period or to more than a limited extent, and the result was that whilst England was giving the foreigner the benefit of free markets she herself was hindered in her export trade by the tariff walls of other countries. Mr. Chamberlain's main remedy was a policy of imperial consolidation—a system of imperial preference, whereby the tariffs of England and her colonies should be so readjusted that discriminating duties were laid upon foreign goods, and preference given by England to colonial and by the colonies to English imports. Thus the trade of England and her colonies would be preserved, in the main, for England and her colonies. This was really an adaptation to new conditions of the old mercantilist colonial policy. But it was sought to commend the idea to free traders by representing it as a movement tending in the direction of freer trade within the Empire.

The protectionist movement once started, however,

became complicated with considerations which had
little or no relation to imperial policy. The introduction of protective tariffs was advocated on the
principle of retaliation against the protective tariffs
of other countries. England, it was urged, by holding
to absolute free trade, had deprived herself of the only
means whereby she could bargain or fight with other
countries for a lowering or removal of their tariff
walls. A tariff that would allow discrimination according to the way in which English imports were treated
by this country or that, might be useful as an instru-
ment in the promotion of universal free trade. Thus
the policy of retaliation was commended as not
inconsistent with the free trade ideal. It was, as it
were, a tariff war to end tariff war. But the arguments for retaliation derived their main appeal less
from the assumed free trade ideal than from that
view of the tariff as a weapon of international strife
which the late Dr. Schmoller noted as a characteristic
feature of the neo-Mercantilism of the twentieth
century.[8] The retaliation doctrine now tended to
become merged in the simple protectionist creed that
England could not successfully contend with other
countries if she did not adopt a system corresponding
to their own. Here there was no talk of a free trade
ideal. It was merely a case of tariff war in a world
of tariff wars. The campaign in short gradually
assumed the character of a call to England to join
in the neo-Mercantilism of the age, and so far as its
advocates went to history for their examples they
always sought them in the mercantilist expedients
whereby, as it was conceived, England had laid the

foundations of her industrial greatness. If England wished to succeed again as she had succeeded in the past, she must, it was said, adopt, with adaptation, the methods that she had then employed. Thus one writer [9] declared that in no system of political economy had the principles of the science been better adapted to the end the nations had in view at the time than in the system of the mercantilists, and the theory of that system must be the guiding principle so long as nations existed as separate entities struggling to maintain each its own individuality in the midst of other States.

The more carefully the subject was considered, however, the more doubtful became both the accuracy of the reading of the situation and the validity of the remedies proposed by the Tariff Reformer. It was true that England had made less relative progress than a few other nations during the previous decade, but this was only what might have been expected. It could hardly have been supposed that she would retain for an indefinite period, for more, indeed, than a considerable number of years, the advantages which she had obtained as the pioneer of the Industrial Revolution. Other countries, later in the field, had been taking their share in improvements from which she had already obtained the maximum benefits, and this fact in itself would tend to produce a change in the relative pace of their economic progress. Moreover, though England had lost her industrial pre-eminence, she retained her supremacy in commerce and navigation, and excelled all other nations in the extent of her capitalistic control.

When the gross volume of English and German foreign trade was examined, it was clear that neither country was now gaining upon the other in the competition for foreign markets.[10] The advance of Germany was mainly on the continent of Europe, and was there obviously due to her geographically central position, her fine railways, and her communications by water with surrounding countries, rather than to any effect of tariff protectionism, whilst England, on the other hand, enjoyed an even greater superiority in trade with the rest of the world by reason of her ocean communications and large and efficient mercantile marine, the prosperity of which was much more obviously connected with the maintenance of free trade. So far as her trade with England was concerned, the growth of Germany's exports seemed to be due rather to her natural resources, the perseverance and enterprise of her people, their study of organization, the application of science to industry, and their capacity for team work than to the fact that the German home market was protected whilst that of England was not.

Similarly, the study of American conditions provided an adequate explanation of her progress to industrial precedence in the large home market available within the territory of the States themselves —a market crossed by no tariff barriers—the energy and inventiveness of the people, and the natural and social conditions, which had enabled America to take the lead in massive production. For her commercial prosperity she was largely dependent upon Great Britain, who not only supplied much capital for her economic development but furnished most of the shipping service for her foreign trade—a·dependence which was to the great advantage of both countries. England had thus been able to obtain the profits of freights, whilst America had been able to devote her energies and capital to activities for which she was much better fitted, economically and geographically, than for shipping.   In the competition for the markets of the United States, England maintained an advantage over all other countries.

So far as England had lost ground, or failed to make ground, from avoidable causes, the general reason was perhaps to be found in an over-complacency engendered by her previous overwhelming pre-eminence. This seemed to have led to a stagnation of inventive faculty, with the result that other countries had come to lead the way in the conception of important inventions or new industrial ideas, or in the adaptation of those ideas to diverse uses and purposes, and particularly in the sphere of technical education. Indeed, the more legitimate conclusion would appear to be, not that adherence to free trade was responsible for the change in England's relative international position, but that it was her free trade which prevented this complacency and stagnation from having so ruinous effect as they might otherwise have done.[11]

So far as the Tariff Reform propaganda depended, as it did depend in its more popular appeals, upon the excess of imports over exports, it reproduced the old fallacy of Mercantilism as to a favourable balance of trade.   It was confronted with an obvious difficulty in the fact that Germany, one of the two great industrial and commercial " enemies," in spite of her protective system, had an unfavourable " balance," and failed to allow for those elements of international indebtedness which helped to make Germany, and still more England, in reality a " creditor " nation, and the United States, in spite of her favourable " balance," a " debtor " nation.   In point of fact, England was importing gold to the extent that the surplus of imported goods failed to make up the balance due to her on account of shipping services, interest on foreign investments, loans, and the like—that is to say, England's earnings by reason of her " invisible exports," as they are not very happily called.   The large surplus of exports from America was but an acknowledgment of indebtedness to other countries, particularly England, representing payment for " invisible imports."

The trained economists did not reproduce the old fallacy, but based their arguments rather on the quality and character of the exports and imports, " visible " or " invisible," as being of importance in relation to national strength and safety apart from their position in the scale of international indebtedness. They pressed the need of self-containedness both for the purpose of independent strength in peace and as a security in time of war.   In short, they criticized the ideal of international division of labour in behalf of the mercantilist aim of national independence. But in this they were setting forward an ideal which was becoming less and less practicable, and which could only be pursued at the risk of diminishing the resources which England actually possessed.

14

The remedies proposed for the disaster under which England was supposed to be suffering were hardly consistent amongst themselves, and it was difficult to see what real gain would follow to either the mother country or the colonies from their adoption. The colonies were willing to grant a preference, but only in such a way as not to interfere with the protection of their own manufactures. On the other hand, inasmuch as free importation existed in England, she could only grant preference, not by admitting colonial products on easier terms than those already obtaining, which was impossible, but by setting up a tariff wherein discrimination was established by making the tax on colonial less than that on foreign commodities. In that case, the imported goods or material, and especially imported food stuffs, would cost more to English consumers. Hence it was not obvious how trade in general, as distinguished from the advantage of particular interests, would be stimulated on one side or the other. Besides, the practice of retaliation between England and foreign countries might at times involve such an arrangement of tariffs as would not be in harmony with the tariff policy of the dominions or the requirements of imperial preference. Further, the abandonment of free trade, the entrance of England into the neo-mercantilist movement, and the setting up of a system of imperial preference and discrimination against foreign countries would inevitably tend to lead other powers to look upon England's vast empire with less acquiescence than heretofore.

The leading economists, with few exceptions, opposed

the movement on both theoretical and practical grounds, and it failed to convert the mass of the people because the disaster for which Tariff Reform was proposed as the only remedy was not evident. Trade was increasing, and the analysis that sought to represent the apparent prosperity as false or unhealthy was lacking in convincing force. So far as social distress existed it seemed to be due not to any inadequacy in the amount of wealth produced under the existing regime but rather to some fault in the manner of its distribution. It was not clear how Tariff Reform would redress that defect. The benefits to be derived from an interference with the free course of trade were problematical, whilst the general rise in prices and particularly in food prices that it would involve seemed a matter of assurance. Hence public opinion had relapsed into indifference to attacks on the fiscal policy. Protectionism seemed to be marking time abroad, and the United States experienced a reaction which brought about a substantial modification of her tariff scale in 1913. The question of Tariff Reform had almost ceased to be a living issue when the Great War broke out, raising issues, both political and economic, more momentous than any that had ever before confronted the nations of Europe and the parts of the world into which Europe had " expanded."

Yet the issues raised by the Great War were not unconnected with those which were in debate during the period of the Tariff Reform controversy. The programme of the movement was but an Anglicized version of the neo-Mercantilism that characterized the policies of other States, and which was partly caused by, and partly helped to accentuate, the elements of international discord that made the outbreak possible. It was the aggressive Mercantilism of Germany that supplied the precipitating force. Both the expansion of her continental borders and that of her extra-European empire were objects dictated primarily by the aims of economic self-sufficiency and independent strength. Her conception of a dominance stretching from the North Sea to the Persian Gulf, maintaining within the area covered a closed, self-sufficient economic system which whilst not under the direct political rule, would be under the virtual control, of Germany as the predominant military power, was essentially mercantilist in character.[12] Nearly all the opponents of Germany shared, in varying degrees, in mercantilist ideas and practices, but in no other country were Mercantilism and imperialism so closely blended in a general policy of power and pursued with so vigorous a resolution. Hence, though the result of the war against one of the two most flourishing protectionist nations was only decided by the entrance into it of the other, the victory of the Allies was in some sort a triumph over the exaggerated mercantilist spirit, which had helped to procure for Germany by its very exaggeration the isolation that spelt her downfall.

And yet, one of the most obvious effects of the war was the renewed life that it gave to mercantilist expedients and policy. In all the countries directly concerned, the State asserted its control on all hands and over all interests, and individual, social, and economic liberty was to a large extent suspended during the term of the struggle. With the British Empire in arms, the idea of its economic independence, with a system of imperial preference, obtained an acceptance which the strenuous propagandist campaign in years of peace had altogether failed to secure for it, and the protection of key and pivotal industries and the formulation of a fighting tariff were the subjects of considered recommendation. The principle of imperial preference, extended to all dutiable articles, was introduced into legislation in the first post-war Budget, and was confirmed in subsequent years. Preferences were already at work in the fiscal relations of the Dominions themselves. The next step was a measure to protect the recently and expensively developed dyestuffs industry by subjecting imports to the requirements of a licence, and this was followed by the Safeguarding of Industries Act, which provided for the imposition of customs duties to protect key and pivotal industries as defined therein, and to combat exchange and other dumping.[13] But unemployment, which had become widespread on the collapse of the post-Armistice boom, and was a deferred consequence of the great upheaval, continued on a large scale, and when a systematic policy of protection and preference, though without the food taxes that Mr. Chamberlain had considered essential to his scheme, was put forward as the only cure, the proposal was decisively rejected by the electorate. The protectionist reaction generated by war and post-war urgencies had indeed gained ·no effective hold upon the minds of the people.[14]

The movement had received some stimulus from an outburst of national protectionism in other countries, arising out of the confusion and difficulties created by the war and the peace settlement, and making itself manifest equally amongst former belligerents and amongst nations that had taken no part in the conflict, equally in countries with low, and those with high, exchanges, equally amongst old States and amongst new, equally in the eastern and in the western hemispheres. The United States devoted to the elaboration and discussion of what was intended to be an adequate customs barrier a larger amount of time than had ever before been given to the preparation of a fiscal measure.[15]   The needs of revenue, the height of prices, the inequality of exchanges, the renewal of competition—all had their shares in the production of the high tariffing, but a strong nationalist spirit, concerned primarily for the safeguarding of home industries, was the main common determinant.

Nevertheless, the war had stressed with unprecedented force the economic interdependence of the nations,[16] and the delusiveness of the mercantilist ideal of self-sufficiency and power ; and the formation of the League of Nations, which had registered the recognition of the necessity of co-operative action in the interests of international peace, might have been regarded as pointing to the emergence of a new temper in the economies of the nations, corresponding to the patent fact of interdependence, and working itself out in an international economic order, such as the trend of history seemed to demand.

The historical development of economic organization

has been marked by so many reversions, overlappings and complications, that any simple statement of sequences is apt to be misleading. It is so much easier to be simple than to be accurate. The phases of national economy itself have been too varied to be rightly the subject of summary generalization. Yet some general conclusions may be drawn from our examination of what has hitherto been its predominant spirit and method.

In the history of one country after another we have traced the appearance and practice of a more or less self-regarding, exclusive economic policy, working through the machinery of the State and in the interests of national power. For manifold reasons, the results have differed widely in different times and in different communities. They have varied according to the character of those who have worked the system, according to the nature of the people amongst whom, and the lands in which, it has been applied, and according to the conditions, in like respects, of competing nations. The ideal is obviously not one which could serve equally well for all, and we have had frequent occasion to observe that the control exercised by State regulations has been far less than it has been usual to suppose, and that they have been largely inoperative, evaded, or defied. It is clear that protective expedients have in many cases had rather the psychological effect of a fetish than the value of actual safeguard, and that their results have often been the reverse of those which they have been meant to produce. Some of the objects of the Mercantilists have been in themselves admirable and common to all wise policy, and it is not difficult to understand, even if we would now criticize, the fundamental mercantilist spirit. Yet we have to say that it has tended to bring about features in economic and political organization and in the management and conduct of international affairs which have had unhappy consequences for the peace of the world. The view that would attribute all the wars of history to purely economic determining causes is out of relation to the complexity of human nature and historical facts, and though we have suggested, we have not elaborated, the connexion between the economic protectionism and economic ambitions of nations and the wars in which they have been engaged, as it has not been possible to state adequately the other elements in a multiplex causation, but there can be no doubt that Mercantilism, being based upon the assumption of international antagonism and strife, has been a potent factor in their perpetuation.

The vogue of neo-Mercantilism has supervened upon, and coincided with, changes which might seem to have provided suggestion for a more illuminated spirit and policy amongst the nations of the world. The enormous development of industry, communication and transport, the vast increase of population, the ever-extending relations of need and supply between different and widely separated parts of the world, have created over its surface an economic unity within which national protective barriers have operated, so far as they have been effective, to check the desirable and necessary flow of international economic intercourse. The due realization of world economy has been hindered by the anachronistic persistence of national protectionism. If old States are to continue doing as they have been wont to do, and new States continue to follow their example, the vision of the new world order must still tarry. But if national economies can shed their anachronistic bias, they may preserve a real and specific surviving value for and in that order. A liberal national economy, combining due freedom for individual enterprise with intelligent social direction, so far from being out of harmony with a true world economy, may be a powerful agent in its service. The League of Nations might perhaps supply the needed connexion between the smaller and the larger economies. As yet the League is rather the significant record of a great ideal than a dominating factor in the counsels of States, but within the limits of its present composition and its present functioning, it has indisputably done good work. Of its strictly political aspect, and its requisite numerical afforcement, we say nothing here. But it has an economic side, on which it has not been idle, and with an extension of its scope in that sphere it might do much to give effect to the lesson of the war, not only by exercising a check upon the erection of national barriers to the essential commerce of the world but by positive co-operative effort for the satisfaction of the world's needs, and by the reasonable application of the principle that the economic life of any specially organized community is at once a dependent and a contributory part of the economic life of universal humanity.

GENERAL BIBLIOGRAPHICAL NOTE

THE best introduction to further reading are W. Cunningham, *Western Civilization in its Economic Aspects*, 2 vols. (1911, 1910), where Mercantilism appears in its historical setting, and G. Schmoller, *The Mercantile System* (1884), tr. by W. J. Ashley (1910), which gives a masterly view of the subject in its widest range and significance. But compare the newer views of economic history in N. S. B. Gras, *Introduction to Economic History* (1922); A. P. Usher, "The Generalizations of Economic History," in *American Journal of Sociology*, XXI, and *Introduction to the Industrial History of England* (1921), c.vi and p. vii.

The history of mercantilist ideas may be followed in such works as L. H. Haney, *History of Economic Thought* (1920), not only in the sections on Mercantilism and Cameralism but in previous and later chapters, and R. Gonnard, *Histoire des doctrines économiques* (1921), which exhibits in the treatment of Mercantilism a strong sense of its bearing at the time of composition. The leading works on the balance-of-trade theory are in German—e.g. E. Heyking, *Zur Geschichte der Handelsbilanztheorie* (1880); H. Schacht, *Der theoretische Gehalt des englischen Merkantilismus* (1910); and L. Petritsch, *Die Theorie von der sogenannten günstigen und ungünstigen Handelsbilanz* (1902)—but we have now also Br. Suviranta, *The Theory of the Balance of Trade in England* (Helsingfors, 1923), dealing with the writers of the XVII and XVIII centuries. T. H. Boggs, *The International Trade Balance in Theory and Practice* (1922) is an up-to-date exposition of the matter.

The course taken by Mercantilism in action may be studied to some extent in general histories, but more adequately in economic histories, as in the relevant portions of C. Day, *History of Commerce* (1922)—the best one-volume survey. G. M. Fisk, *International Commercial Policies* (1907), will also be found useful. For ampler consultation there is the French series which includes G. Glotz, *Le Travail dans la Grèce ancienne* (1920)—the best economic history of Greece ; P. Louis, *Le Travail dans le monde romain* (1912) ; P. Boissonade, *Le Travail dans l'Europe chrétienne au moyen âge* (1921) ; G. Renard and G. Weulersse, *Le Travail dans l'Europe moderne* (1920); L. Capitan et H. Lorin, *Le Travail en Amérique* (1914); B. Nogaro et W. Oualid, *L'Évolution du commerce et du crédit depuis cent cinquante ans* (1914), and G. Renard et A. Dulac, *L'Évolution industrielle et agricole depuis cent cinquante ans* (1912). But the amount and value of the relevant matter in the different volumes varies considerably. References for the different countries will be given in the chapter-notes, but two works in English economic history are mentioned here because of their special importance for our subject—W. Cunningham, *Growth of English Industry and Commerce*, 2 vols. (I, ed. 1915 ; II, Pt. I, ed. 1919, Pt. II, ed. 1917—continuously paged), and G. Unwin, *Industrial Organisation in the XVI and XVII Centuries* (1904). Cunningham's treatment of Mercantilism is sympathetic, though critical. Professor Unwin is strongly anti-Mercantilist. For the XIX and XX centuries two volumes which bear directly on our subject are C. F. Bastable, *Commerce of Nations*, revised T. E. Gregory (1923), dealing with the theory and history of commercial policy to 1922 ; and A. Viallate, *Economic Imperialism* (1923), which surveys the changes in economic conditions and policies during the last fifty years. J. Grunzel, *Economic Protectionism* (1916) is an informative, judicial study by an Austrian scholar. C. Gill, *National Power and Prosperity*, with an Introduction by Professor Unwin, is a vigorous and able criticism of the mercantilist ideas of national interests and power.

The notes to the chapters point to works which may be consulted on the special topics presented therein. The following contractions are used :

A.H.R. : *American Historical Review. C.M.H.* : *Cambridge Modern History. D.P.E.* : *Dictionary of Political Economy*, ed. R. H. Palgrave. *E.H.R.* : *English Historical Review. E.J.* : *Economic Journal. Select Documents* : Bland, Brown and Tawney, *English Economic History— Select Documents.*

NOTES

CHAPTER I

[1] In the *New English Dictionary* " Mercantile System " is explained as a term used by Adam Smith and later political economists " for the system of economic doctrine and legislative policy based on the principle that money alone constituted wealth," and quotations are given to support this definition, which, however, is quite inadequate. A suggestion of the larger meaning is afforded by a quotation from Cunningham under " Mercantilist " : " The mercantilists held that the direction in which capital was used should be controlled so that the power of the state might be maintained."

[2] Adam Smith called it indifferently the system of commerce, the commercial system, or the mercantile system (*Wealth of Nations*, ed. Cannan, I, pp. 395, 401).

[3] F. List, *National System of Political Economy*, tr. Lloyd (1904), pp. 269, 276, 280, 283.

[4] Jean Baptiste Colbert, minister of Louis XIV.

[5] See W. A. S. Hewins in *D.P.E.*, II, p. 727a.

CHAPTER II

[1] For ancient economic ideas see—in addition to works mentioned in the general note—A. A. Trever, *History of Greek Economic Thought* (1916), and E. Simey, " Economic Theory among the Greeks and Romans," *Economic Review*, X, pp. 462 *sq.*, 1900. But note Cunningham's remark that the principles of the Mercantile System do not ¡ been clearly formulated in ancient time *tion*, I, p. 138 n.).

[2] See especially F. M. Cornford, (1907) ; G. B. Grundy, *Thucydides* (1911).

[3] This is emphasized by Glotz in *Le Travail dans la Grèce ancienne*.

[4] For Carthaginian policy see S. Gsell, *Histoire ancienne de l'Afrique du Nord*, II (1913).

[5] G. Ferrero, *The Greatness and Decline of Rome*, I, tr. from Italian (1907), pp. vi, 43.

[6] References to typical passages in Mommsen, Wilamowitz Moellendorff, Colin, Ferrero, and Heitland are given by Tenney Frank in his *Roman Imperialism* (1914), p. 277.

[7] See remarks by W. S. Ferguson and others in discussion on the economic causes of international rivalries and wars in ancient times (American Historical Association's *Annual Report for 1915* (1917), pp. 34, 35, 113 *sq.*).

[8] See Tenney Frank, *Roman Imperialism*, c. xiv; N. Baynes, " Rome's Foreign Policy and Trade Interests," *History*, New Series, II, pp. 238 *sq.* ; G. W. Botsford in discussion referred to above. G. Salvioli, in *Le Capitalisme dans le monde antique*, tr. from Italian (1906), strongly attacks the " modernizing " of ancient history in its economic aspects, but is too much under the influence of the Marxian view of the late appearance of Capitalism.

[9] See W. L. Westerman, " The Economic Basis of the Decline of Ancient Culture," *A.H.R.*, XX, p. 728.

[10] See W. A. Brown, " State Control of Industry in the IV Century," *Political Science Quarterly*, II, pp. 494 *sq.*

CHAPTER III

[1] For mediaeval ideas, see V. Brants, *L'Économie politique au moyen âge* (1895), and G. O'Brien, *Essay on Mediaeval Economic Theory* (1920).

[2] Aristotle ostensibly bases his argument on the fact that the Greek word for " interest " means child, as if to say that interest was the child of the principal. Coin can have no progeny. Therefore, he urges, money derived from the loan of money is an unnatural acquisition (*Politics*, I, x, 4, 5). For this manner of appeal to etymology and the influence of Aristotle's economic theory in the Middle Ages, see E. Barker, *The Political Thought of Plato and Aristotle* (1906), pp. 387–90.

But Trever suggests that the etymological argument was not intended seriously (*Greek Economic Thought*, p. 35).

³ For this phase of economic policy see P. Imbart de la Tour, *La Liberté commerciale en France aux XII* et XIII* siècles* (1895).

⁴ W. J. Ashley, *Introduction to English Economic History and Theory*, II (1913), p. 379, introducing a valuable chapter.

⁵ For the work and importance of Nicholas Oresme, a French scholar of the XIV century, see Cunningham, *Industry and Commerce*, I, pp. 355–9, but on the question of originality cp. *D.P.E.*, III, p. 43.

⁶ For urban economy, compare Schmoller and Cunningham with Gras and Usher, in works mentioned on p. 219.

⁷ List's chapter on the Italians in his *National System* is concerned mainly with Venice. Cp. Marshall, *Industry and Trade*, pp. 687–8, and his criticism of List's explanation of her decline.

⁸ J. N. Figgis, *C.M.H.*, III, p. 736.

⁹ A. F. Pollard, *History of England* (1912), p. 94.

¹⁰ For the influence of Humanism and of Protestant thought on economic opinion and practice, see *D.P.E.*, I, pp. 337–9, 285–6. M. L. Hennebicq finds the genesis of English imperialism, political and economic, in the Protestant interpretation of the Bible (*Genèse de l'imperialisme anglais*, 1913); Dr. Cunningham remarks on the alliance of Calvinism and Capitalism (*Christianity and Economic Science*, 1914, c. 5); and Dr. G. O'Brien makes Protestantism responsible for both Capitalism and Socialism (*Essay on the Economic Effects of the Reformation*, 1923); but the tendency in these essays is to attribute too much to Protestantism, both directly and indirectly.

¹¹ Machiavelli, *Discourses*, Bk. II, c. 10, is devoted to this proposition.

CHAPTER IV

¹ Cp. N. S. B. Gras, *Evolution of the English Corn Market* (1915), on the metropolitan market in the XVI and XVII centuries.

² For the English town economy, see W. J. Ashley, *Intro-*
15

duction, I, c. 2, and II, c. 1; Mrs. J. R. Green, *Town Life in the XV Century* (1894); E. Lipson, *Economic History of England*, I (1915), c. vii; and compare Usher, *Industrial History of England*, c. vi, on the subject.

[3] For illustration of this policy in the early XVII century, see *Assembly Books of Southampton*, ed. Horrocks, I and II, Introductions.

[4] Professor Gras has put forward the theory that national customs dues were founded on a model provided by the towns (*The Early English Customs System*, 1918, p. 21). But note Professor Unwin's criticism, *History*, IV, pp. 222-3.

[5] The view taken by H. Heaton, in *The Yorkshire Woollen and Worsted Industries* (1920). H. G. Gray, writing of the industry generally, is of much the same opinion (*E.H.R.*, XXXIX, pp. 22-3, 33).

[6] This is amply illustrated by Heaton. See also E. Lipson, *History of the Woollen and Worsted Industries* (1921).

[7] For Aylesbury's opinion in full, see *Select Documents*, p. 222.

[8] The best explanation of the " balance of bargains " is in Richard Jones, " Essay on Primitive Political Economy in England," *Edinburgh Review*, LXXXV.

[9] " The Libel of English Policy" (*Political Poems and Songs*, ed. T. Wright, II, pp. 160 *sq.*; extracts in *England under the Lancastrians*, ed. J. H. Flemming, 1921, pp. 251-3; summary with quotations in E. Lipson, *Economic History of England*, 1915, pp. 499-501) and " On England's Commercial Policy " (*Political Poems*, II, pp. 282 *sq.*; extract in *England under the Yorkists*, ed. I D. Thornley, 1920, pp. 198-9; notice in Lipson, *Economic History*, pp. 422-3, 501).

[10] *Discourse of the Common Weal of this Realm of England*, probably written by John Hales in 1549; edited by Miss E. Lamond in 1893; extracts in *Select Documents*, pp. 404 *sq.*

[11] Cp. Hewins, *D.P.E.*, II, pp. 590-1. The best account of the policy is in Cunningham, *Industry and Commerce*, II, pp. 25 *sq.*

[12] See W. H. Price, *English Patents of Monopoly* (1906), pp. 128-32.

[13] *Select Charters of Trading Companies*, ed. C. T. Carr (1913), pp. xxiv, xxv.

[14] See O. C. Dunlop, " Some Aspects of Early English

Apprenticeship," *Transactions*, Royal Historical Society, 3rd series, V, pp. 193–4.

[15] See Gras, *Evolution of the English Corn Market*, pp. 221 *sq.*

[16] W. R. Scott, *Constitution and Finance of English Joint Stock Companies to 1720*, I (1910), pp. 88–91.

CHAPTER V

[1] For this petition, *Select Documents*, pp. 443 *sq.* As to XVI century companies generally, Hewins, *English Trade and Finance* (1892), esp. pp. 72–3, takes an unfavourable view. Scott, *Joint Stock Companies*, I, c. xxiii, has more to say in behalf of the joint stock type.

[2] For this matter see *Select Charters*, ed. Carr, pp. lxvii–lxviii, 78 *sq.* ; *Select Documents*, pp. 454–62 ; Hewins, *Trade and Finance*, pp. 102 *sq.* ; G. Unwin, *Industrial Organisation in the XVI and XVII Centuries* (1904), pp. 172 *sq.*

[3] List, *National System*, pp. 30–1.

[4] For Wentworth's own account of his policy, *Select Documents*, pp. 470–2.

[5] According to F. Strong, *A.H.R.*, IV, p. 231, Cromwell was " immersed in the mercantile system of the time."

[6] See List's view of the results of the Navigation Act (*National System*, pp. 33–4).

[7] F. Strong, *The Causes of Cromwell's West Indian Policy*, *A.H.R.* IV, pp. 228–45.

[8] The matter is discussed with references by G. N. Clark, "The Navigation Act of 1651," in *History*, VII, pp. 282 *sq.* In Cunningham, *Industry and Commerce*, see II, pp. 210–13.

[9] Scott, *Joint Stock Companies*, I, pp. 250 *sq.* ; Cunningham, *Industry and Commerce*, II, pp. 186–7.

[10] On the view of Cromwell as an imperialist, see Cunningham, *Industry and Commerce*, II, pp. 193–4, with references.

[11] For the financial effects of the war with Spain, see Scott, *Joint Stock Companies*, I, pp. 260–2.

[12] Thomas Mun (1571–1641), a London merchant of much repute, was a director of the East India Company, and member of the standing committee on trade, appointed in 1622 and reappointed in 1625, which was the origin of the

Board of Trade. The work that was to make his name famous —*England's Treasure by Forraign Trade, Or, The Balance of Our Forraign Trade is the Rule of our Treasure*—written within 1622–8, was not published till twenty-three years after his death (1664). The most convenient edition is that by W. J. Ashley (1895).

[13] See Sir W. Ashley's Introduction for these estimates.

[14] For the views of these writers, see Hewins, *Trade and Finance*, Introduction ; Cunningham, *Industry and Commerce*, II, pp. 380–402, and especially, Suviranta, *The Theory of the Balance of Trade in England* (1923), and E. S. Furness, *The Position of the Laborer in a System of Nationalism : A Study in the Labor Theories of the later English Mercantilists* (1920).

[15] The best account of English Mercantilism is in Cunningham, *Industry and Commerce*, esp. I, pp. 467–72, 481–3, and II, pp. 13–24, but his view of Edward III should be considered in the light of Professor Unwin's Introduction to *Finance and Trade under Edward III* (1918). See also Marshall on English Mercantilism in *Industry and Trade*, App. D.

[16] *England's Treasure*, cc. 2, 8–14.

[17] See Cunningham, *Industry and Commerce*, II, pp. 396 *sq.* ; Suviranta, *Balance of Trade*, pp. 141 *sq.*

[18] J. Tucker, *The Elements of Commerce* (1755), p. 103.

[19] In his *Discourse of Trade from England into the East Indies* (1621), and *England's Treasure*, c. 4.

[20] On this subject see remarks and notes (v. 8) on the Ordinance of 1651, and the article on the Navigation Laws, *D.P.E.*, III, esp. pp. 10–11.

[21] John Adams (1735–1836), who helped to draw up the Declaration of Independence (1776), and succeeded Washington as President (1797).

[22] Notably by the late Professor H. L. Osgood and the late Mr. G. L. Beer in their elucidation of England's colonial policy in the XVII and XVIII centuries. For general American accounts on the revised lines see S. G. Fisher, *The True History of the American Revolution* (1902) and C. H. Van Tyne, *The Causes of the War of Independence* (1922). The most notable English contributor to the revised view is Sir W J. Ashley, in " The English Commercial Legislation and the American Colonies 1660–1760," and " American

Smuggling, 1660–1760 " (Surveys, Historic and Economic, 1900). The most recent English survey is by H. E. Egerton, The Causes and Character of the American Revolution (1923).

[23] See F. W. Pitman, The Development of the British West Indies 1700–1763 (1917), on this subject.

[24] See E. B. Greene, The Provincial Governors in the English Colonies of North America (1898), pp. 203–5.

[25] For the sugar question, see Pitman, British West Indies; also C. M. Andrews, " Anglo-French Commercial Rivalry," A.H.R., XX.

[26] The main argument of H. Thatcher in his paper, The True Cause of the American Revolution (1920). A valuable study of the question of expansion in its bearing on the Revolution is C. W. Alvord, The Mississippi Valley in American Politics (1917)—cp. II, pp. 249 sq.

[27] Well brought out in A. M. Schlesinger, Colonial Merchants and the American Revolution (1918).

[28] See T. Keith, Commercial Relations of England and Scotland, 1603–1707 (1910), on the subject of this paragraph.

[29] Reference may be made to A. E. Murray, History of the Commercial and Financial Relations between England and Ireland from the period of the Restoration (1903) ; G. O'Brien, The Economic History of Ireland in the XVIII Century (1918), and The Economic History of Ireland in the XVII Century (1919).

[30] For the anti-French Mercantilism, see Hewins, Trade and Finance, pp. 133–44, W. J. Ashley, " The Tory Origins of Free Trade," in Surveys; D. G. Hall, " Anglo-French Relations under Charles II," History, VII, pp. 17–30 ; L. B. Packard, " International Rivalry and Free Trade Origins, 1660–1678," Quarterly Journal of Economics, May, 1923. In The Dutch Alliance and the War against French Trade 1688–1697, Mr. G. N. Clark shows the failure of the attempt from the point of view of the allies. C. M. Andrews, " Anglo-French Commercial Rivalry, 1700–1750—Western Phase," A.H.R., X, is based largely upon the writings of XVIII century mercantilist pamphleteers.

[31] See Hewins, Trade and Finance, pp. 129–37; A. B. Wallis Chapman, " The Commercial Relations of England and Portugal," in Transactions, R. Hist. S., 3rd series, I, pp. 157 sq.

[82] *Wealth of Nations*, ed. Cannan, II, pp. 47–50.

[83] List, *National System*, pp. 34, 49–54.

[84] *Transactions*. R. Hist. S., 3rd series, I, p. 178 ; *D.P.E.*, II, p. 748.

[85] On these points cp. Schmoller, *Mercantile System*, pp. 64 *sq.* ; Wakeman, *Ascendancy of France*, pp. 202–3 ; J. W. Welsford, *Strength of England* (1910), pp. 349–50.

[86] Seeley, *Expansion of England* (ed. 1899), p. 129.

[87] See Gras, *Evolution of the Corn Market*, p. 254, and Hewins, E. J., II, p. 698, for the view presented as against that of Cunningham.

CHAPTER VI

[1] For these writers and the conditions under which they put forward their views, see Ashley, Hall, and Packard as in note v, 30. The most notable were Sir Dudley North (1641–90) and Nicholas Barbon (1640?–1698), perhaps son of Praisegod Barebon.

[2] The mercantilist features of Walpole's economic policy are emphasized—perhaps over-emphasized—by H. W. V. Temperley in *C.M.H.*, VI, pp. 49–56.

[3] The term Physiocrats was meant to indicate that the system was based upon the law of nature and not upon the regulations of man. The founder was Quesnay (1694–1774), physician to Louis XV. See H. Higgs, *The Physiocrats* (1897) ; G. Weulersse, *Le Mouvement physiocratique en France* (1910) ; C. Gide and C. Rist, *History of Economic Theories from the Physiocrats to our Own Time*, tr. (1905) ; and the *D.P.E.* under " Économistes," " Physiocrats," and the names of persons mentioned.

[4] Adam Smith (1729–90) was a Fifeshire man, educated at Glasgow and Oxford, successively Professor of Logic and of Moral Philosophy at Edinburgh, and finally Commissioner of Customs at Edinburgh. For an admirable summary of his work, and other particulars, see *D.P.E.*, III, pp. 412 *sq.* The best recent editions are by Dr. E. Cannan and Dr. W. R. Scott.

[5] See Cunningham, " Economic Doctrine in the XVIII Century," *E.J.*, I, for this line of criticism.

[8] As List does (*National System*, p. 97). For a corrective see Professor J. W. Nicholson, *ib.*, Introduction, p. xiv, and on " The Nationalism of Adam Smith " in *A Project of Empire* (1909) ; also Marshall, *Industry and Trade*, pp. 746–7.

[7] Cf. Nicholson, *A Project of Empire*, cc. 14, 15, 16. On the general subject of the paragraph, reference may be made to L. L. Price on " Adam Smith in Relation to Recent Economics," in *Economic Science and Practice* (1896), and on " Free Trade and Protection," *E.J.*, XII (1902).

[8] See Hewins, *Trade and Finance*, pp. 144–58 ; Witt Bowden, " The English Manufacturers and the Commercial Treaty with France," *A.H.R.*, XXV, pp. 18 *sq.*

[9] For these petitions and their sequel see *Select Documents,* pp. 698–701, and L. Levi, *History of British Commerce* (1880), pp. 152 *sq.* The London petition was drawn up by Thomas Tooke, whom the late Sir Robert Giffen once described as " the greatest economist the country has had."

[10] On the Free Trade movement, in addition to Cunningham, reference may be made to *D.P.E.*, II, pp. 146 *sq.* ; A. Mongredien, *History of the Free Trade Movement in England* (1881) ; G. Armitage-Smith, *The Free Trade Movement and its Results* (1903) ; B. Holland, *The Fall of Protection 1840–1850* (1913).

CHAPTER VII

[1] For this view, see E. G. Bourne, *Spain in America* (1904), pp. 211 *sq.*, 239–42. Other works in which Spanish Mercantilism may be studied are W. G. F. Roscher, *The Spanish Colonial System*, tr. (1904) ; C. H. Haring, *Trade and Navigation between Spain and the Indies in the Time of the Hapsburgs* (1918) ; J. Klein, *The Mesta : A Study in Spanish Economic History, 1273–1836* (1920) ; and C. E. Chapman, *History of Spain* (1918), esp. cc. 15, 28, 37.

[2] For Uztariz (1670–1732) and his work see A. Wirminghaus, *Zwei Spanische Mercantilisten—Uztariz und Ulloa* (1886), or, better, A. Mounier, *Les Faits et la doctrine économiques en Espagne sous Philippe V : Geronimo de Uztariz* (1919), and M. Boissonade's review article in *Revue historique*, Nov.– Dec., 1919.

[3] Cf. references to Uztariz by List, *National System*, pp. 47, 54.

[4] For Campomanes (1723–1802), jurist, economist, and statesman, see G. Desdevises du Dezert, *Les Lettres politico-économiques de C.* (1897).

[5] See F. A. Kirkpatrick, in *C.M.H.*, X, pp. 244 *sq.*, and esp. 276–9.

[6] For Holland the relevant passages in P. J. Blok, *History of the People of the Netherlands*, 5 vols. (1898–1912) ; J. T. Rogers, *Holland* (1889) ; or G. Edmundson, *History of Holland* (1922) may be consulted. The most valuable work in English on Dutch economic policy is C. Day, *The Dutch in Java* (1904). See also Marshall, *Industry and Trade*, pp. 689–96. For economic thought, see E. Laspeyres, *Geschichte der volkswirth-schaftlichen Anschauungen der Niederlander* (1863).

[7] For opinions on causes see Cunningham, *Western Civiliza-tion*, II, pp. 203–6, and *Industry and Commerce*, II, pp. 675–6 n.; List, on the Netherlands, in the *National System* ; and Wels-ford, *Strength of Nations*, pp. 148 *sq.*

[8] Note the important observations by Marshall, *Industry and Trade*, p. 699.

[9] From this point we have A. Heringa, *Free Trade and Protection in Holland* (1914), and Day, *The Dutch in Java*, cc. 6–12.

CHAPTER VIII

[1] There is no general account in English of French economic history and policy over any large period before the XIX century. In French the works of E. Levasseur, *Histoire des classes ouvrières et de l'industrie en France*, and Pigeonneau, *Histoire du commerce de la France*, may be consulted. Imbart de la Tour, *La Liberté commerciale en France aux XIIe et XIIIe siècles* (1895) is good on economic policy for a much longer period than is indicated by the title. A. Schatz and R. Caillemer, *Le Mercantilisme libéral à la fin du XVIIe siècle* (1906), review economic policy down to the time mentioned. A. P. Usher, *History of the Grain Trade in France, 1400–1710*, throws much light on economic policy and conditions.

[2] The mercantilist aspects of Richelieu's aims and work

receive special attention in F. C. Palm, *The Economic Policies of Richelieu* (1922).

[3] Jean Baptiste Colbert (1619–1683), son of a wool merchant, became servant of Cardinal Mazarin, who on his death-bed recommended him to Louis XIV. He was made intendant of finances, and on the fall of Fouqué succeeded him as superintendent (1661), afterwards becoming controller general. His work in its best features was largely thwarted by his master's military ambition and the consequent ascendancy of Louvois, secretary for war. Good accounts of his policy are A. J. Sargent, *The Economic Policy of Colbert* (1899) ; S. L. Mims, *Colbert's West Indian Policy* (1912) ; A. J. Grant, *C.M.H.*, V, pp. 6 *sq.* ; H. O. Wakeman, *The Ascendancy of France*, pp. 197–203 ; Marshall, *Industry and Trade*, pp. 739–41.

[4] He was doubtless also influenced by Montchrétien, author of a *Traicté de l'Œconomie Politique* (1615), the first work issued as on that subject, but containing little that was original.

[5] See List, *National System*, pp. 57–8, 93, 274, 276.

[6] See Usher, *Grain Trade in France*, pp. 268 *sq.*

[7] Note Wakeman's observations on this war as a landmark in the connexion of protectionism and war in the later XVII and the XVIII centuries (*Ascendancy of France*, pp. 202–3.)

[8] Cp. J. W. Thompson, " Some Economic Factors in the Revocation of the Edict of Nantes," *A.H.R.*, XIV.

[9] For an appreciation of Law (1671–1728), see J. S. Nicholson, *A Treatise on Money* (1903), pp. 165 *sq.*

[10] For these men and their views, see Schatz and Caillemer, *Le Mercantilisme libéral, &c., Les Idées économiques et politiques du M. de Belesbat* (1906).

[11] See note vi, 3.

[12] For Turgot (1727–81) reference may be made to the appreciative account in the *D.P.E.*

[13] Against List, *National System*, pp. 59, 259, 296, as to alleged ill effects in France, see Levasseur, *Histoire . . . avant 1789*, II, (1901), pp. 563–5, and Hewins, *Trade and Finance*, pp. 55–6.

[14] The subject has been recently studied in F. E. Melvin, *Napoleon's Navigation System* (1919), and E. F. Heckscher, *The Continental System* (1922).

[15] From this point we have P. Ashley, *Modern Tariff History* (1920), cc. on France ; H. O. Meredith, *Protection in France* (1904) ; and J. H. Clapham, *The Economic Development of France and Germany 1815–1914* (1921).

[16] Frédéric Bastiat (1801–1850), author of the famous *Economic Sophisms*.

[17] See Levi, *History of British Commerce*, pp. 417 sq., for the Franco-British and other commercial treaties.

[18] Cp. Marshall, *Industry and Trade*, p. 120. The whole chapter is important.

[19] Note M. Caillaux's suggestion and Suviranta's comment, *Balance of Trade*, p. 156 n.

[20] A Girault, *The Colonial Tariff Policy of France* (1916), for the subject of this paragraph.

CHAPTER IX

[1] For German conditions in the XV and XVI centuries reference may be made to the translation of J. Janssen's voluminous work, *History of the German People at the Close of the Middle Ages*, esp. on commerce and capital, II, pp. 43 sq., the Holy Roman Empire, II, pp. 105 sq. ; and on economic conditions in XV.

[2] On this scheme, see Janssen, *German People*, III, pp. 317–19, and IV, pp. 15–19, 29 ; E. Armstrong, *Charles V*, I, (1910) pp. 203–4. For the treatment of the matter as affording a striking example of the ruinous effects of the rejection of "Tariff Reform," see Welsford, *Strength of Nations* (1907), cc. 12, 13.

[3] Janssen, *German People*, XV, p. 21.

[4] On the effects of the Thirty Years War, "perhaps the most appalling demonstration of the consequences of war to be found in history," as he then expressed himself, see the late Sir A. W. Ward's article in *C.M.H.*, IV, pp. 471 sq.

[5] We have an excellent account of them by A. W. Small, *The Cameralists—The Pioneers of German Social Polity* (1909). Seckendorff (1626–92), Justi (1720–71), and Sonnenfels (1733–1817) are the most notable. Another, Schröder

(*d.* 1689) spent many years in England, and shows the influence of Mun's work. For Hornig, whose book Small had not seen, reference may be made to Haney, *Economic Thought*, pp. 141–4.

⁶ For this subject, see Schmoller, *Mercantile System*, pp. 56–7, 81–91, and the original German work ; Haney, *Economic Thought*, pp. 134–5 ; E. Daniels, *C.M.H.*, VI, c. 8, esp. pp. 208, 224–5, and c. 20, esp. pp. 718–23.

⁷ See *C.M.H.*, VI, pp. 722–3.

⁸ *De la monarchie prussienne sous Frédéric le Grand* (London, 1788).

⁹ For Stein (1757–1831) we have ample matter in Sir J. R. Seeley, *Life and Times of Stein* (1878), and G. S. Ford, *Stein and the Era of Reform in Prussia* (1922).

¹⁰ From this point we have P. Ashley, *Modern Tariff History*, chapters on Germany ; W. H. Dawson, *Protection in Germany* (1904), and *The Evolution of Germany* (1919) ; and J. H. Clapham, *The Economic Development of France and Germany*.

¹¹ Adam Heinrich Müller (1779–1829), who, though criticizing Adam Smith, counted him " the greatest writer of all times in political economy."

¹² Friedrich List (1787–1846), founder of " scientific protection," was a native of Würtemberg, entered the public service, became ministerial under-secretary, and afterwards professor at Tübingen, but his activity in the movement aiming at the abolition of internal duties and the establishment of a customs union for Germany and in the advocacy of other reforms brought about the loss of his chair. He was elected to the legislative assembly, but, continuing to press for reforms, was expelled, imprisoned, and finally exiled. He went to America, where he gained success both in financial speculations and in journalism, and published *Outlines of American Political Economy* (1827) which contains the principal ideas of his later work. Returning to Europe he served the U.S. first on a mission to Paris and afterwards as consul at Leipzig. He threw his main energies into the advocacy in the Press and otherwise of national economic development in Germany. In 1841 he published *The National System of Political Economy*, intended to be the first of a work in three parts, but his ceaseless labours undermined his health and he died by his own hand at Augsburg in 1846. List

deserves more than anyone else the title of " creator " of the Zollverein, and he has perhaps had more influence than any other writer on the protectionist movement generally. The translation of *The National System* by S. S. Lloyd contains a short memoir by the translator and an Introduction by Professor J. W. Nicholson. See also the article on List in the *D.P.E.* List is treated in relation to the American protectionists, Hamilton and Carey, by U. Rabbeno in *American Commercial Policy*, tr. (1895).

[13] On the faults of the Mercantile System, see *National System*, p. 272, and for List's defence against the charge that he was " merely seeking to revive the (so-called) ' mercantile system,' " see p. xliii.

[14] *National System*, p. 341.

[15] Note the remarks on the Bismarckian and mercantilist doctrine of power by C. G. Robertson, *Bismarck* (1918), p. 416.

[16] For German methods of commercial expansion and penetration, see H. Hauser, *Germany's Commercial Grip on the World*, tr. (1918).

[17] Marshall, *Industry and Trade*, p. 134. The whole chapter on the industrial leadership of Germany is important. See also Appendix F.

[18] For a striking criticism of the " New Mercantilism " in Germany by a German writer, see W. Lotz, " The Effect of Protection on some German Industries," *E.J.*, XIV (1904).

[19] Cp. Marshall, *Industry and Trade*, p. 853, on German wages before the Great War.

CHAPTER X

[1] Joseph II, who reigned 1765–90, is said to have been greatly impressed by Hornig's *Oesterreich uber alles wann es nur will* (1684)—" Austria over all if she only will "—which urged that by following the economic methods of France, Holland, and England, by exploiting all her resources, excluding foreign manufactures, and the like, she might surpass any other European State in power and wealth (*D.P.E.*, II, p. 331 ; Haney, *Economic Thought*, pp. 141–2). Joseph had

physiocratic notions in some directions, but in others he was decidedly mercantilist and Colbertian (*C.M.H.*, VI, p. 639).

² For this scheme and Austria's relation to it, see A. Zimmern, *Nationality and Government* (1919), pp. 309 *sq.*, and Ramsay Muir, *Expansion of Europe* (1922), pp. 246 *sq.*

³ For Cavour's economic views in his own words, see *D.P.E.*, I, pp. 234-7.

⁴ For these countries, see P. Drachmann, *The Industrial Development and Commercial Policies of the Three Scandinavian Countries* (1915), and H. L. Westergaard, *The Economic Development in Denmark before and during the World War* (1922).

⁵ For economic thought and history in Russia see *D.P.E.*, III, pp. 336 *sq.*; J. Mavor, *Economic History of Russia* (1914); K. Leites, *Recent Economic Development in Russia* (1922).

⁶ See Pernet, *Pierre le Grand Mercantiliste* (1913), for a full account of his work. List's chapter on the Russians may be noted here.

⁷ As to the " great " Catherine, who had liberal views, but veered round to protection, see *C.M.H.*, VI, pp. 691-2.

⁸ Heinrich Friedrich von Storch (1766–1835), *D.P.E.*, III, p. 479.

⁹ See Trevor Johnes, " Notes on the Social and Economic Transition in Japan," *E.J.*, XXXI, pp. 50 *sq.*

¹⁰ Cp. T. H. Sanders, " Japan's Financial Opportunities," *E.J.*, XXVI; J. Soyeda, " Effect of the War on Japanese Finance " (*ib.*, XXVI), and " The Economic Situation in Japan " (*ib.*, XXXIII); J. H. Longford, " Japan's Economic Independence."

CHAPTER XI

¹ Alexander Hamilton (1757–1804) was born in the West Indies and educated at New York. As a youth of eighteen he wrote a pamphlet in support of the cause of the colonists against the mother country, and during the war, after starting as captain of artillery, he served for several years as aide-de-camp to Washington. On his return to civil life he became a lawyer in New York, and in 1782 he was elected to Congress.

He took a prominent part in the discussions on the constitution, and was the initiator of, and chief contributor to, the *Federalist* series of essays—the most notable work in American political literature. As secretary of the Treasury department, appointed in 1789, he was responsible for its first organization, and in his " Report on the Encouragement of Manufactures," prepared under the direction of Congress, and issued on 5th December, 1791, he gave what Professor Taussig, himself of Free Trade sympathies, regards as " the strongest presentation of the case for protection which has been made by an American statesman." The full text of the Report is in *State Papers and Speeches on the Tariff*, edited by F. W. Taussig (1893). Hamilton resigned in 1795, and returned to the practice of law, but he was leader of the federal party till his death, which occurred as the result of a duel with a political opponent. There are books on him by H. C. Lodge (1882), W. G. Sumner (1901), F. S. Oliver (1906), W. S. Culbertson (1911), and F S. Scott (6th ed. 1915). A significant recent title is A. H. Vandenberg, *The Greatest American : Alexander Hamilton* (1922). For a discussion of his views on protection see Rabbeno, *American Commercial Policy*.

  [2] This is Sumner's view.

  [3] For the protectionist movement in the U.S. see E. L. Bogart, *Economic History of the U.S.* (1912) ; H. C. Emery, " The Economic Development of the U.S.," *C.M.H.*, VII, c. 22 ; F. W. Taussig, *Tariff History of the U.S.* (1914) ; P. Ashley, *Modern Tariff History*, chapters on America.

  [4] This is Taussig's opinion. See also Marshall, *Industry and Commerce*, pp. 773–84.

  [5] George McDuffie, of South Carolina, speaking in 1830.

  [6] Henry Charles Carey (1793-1879), born at Philadelphia, son of Matthew Carey, publisher and advocate of protection. Henry entered his father's business, and in 1821 became sole manager. He retired in 1835, and devoted himself entirely to study and writing on social, economic, and political science. His literary output was large, and his leading works were translated into several languages. He summed up his views in his *Principles of Social Science* (1858-9), which was issued in condensed form as *The Manual of Social Science*, ed. by K. McKean (1864). In later years he has attracted far less attention than Hamilton, but note D. H. Mason, *Time's*

Vindication of H. C. Carey (1891). For the main points in his views, see Rabbeno, *American Commercial Policy*, and Haney, *Economic Thought*.

[7] See Marshall, *Industry and Trade*, pp.' 140 *sq.*, and 773 *sq.*, as to the causes of American industrial progress.

[8] Edward N. Dingley, son of Dingley of the Tariff, in *Proceedings of the Academy of Political Science in the City of New York*, IX (1920–2), p. 175.

[9] The attempt to afford discrimination by giving more favourable railway rates to goods imported or to be exported in American bottoms has had to be abandoned for the present.

[10] For American views as summarized in the preceding paragraphs, cp. *Proceedings of the Academy of Political Science of New York*, IX, the whole of Pt. 2 ; also C. M. Pepper, *American Foreign Trade* (1919).

[11] Cp. S. P. Triana, on the international position of the South American countries, *C.M.H.*, XII, pp. 689 *sq.*

[12] See F. R. Rutter, *The Tariff Systems of South American Countries* (1916), on this point.

CHAPTER XII

[1] For its history, see S. J. Maclean, *The Tariff History of Canada* (1895) ; E. Porritt, *Sixty Years of Protection in Canada, 1846–1907* (1908), and *The Revolt in Canada against the New Feudalism, Tariff History, 1907–1910* (1911) ; C. Chomley, *Protection in Canada and Australasia* (1904).

[2] Illustrated in C. D. Allin, *A History of the Tariff Relations of the American Colonies* (1918).

[3] Ambrose Pratt, *David Syme*, (1908). For the general movement, cp. Chomley, and H. Heaton, *Modern Economic History, with special reference to Australia* (1922).

[4] For an explanation of the " New Protection," as it is called in Australia, see *Official Yearbook of the Commonwealth of Australia* for 1916, p. 967, and Heaton, pp. 101–2.

[5] P. Banerjea, in *Fiscal Policy in India* (1922).

[6] H. B. Lees Smith, in *India and the Tariff Problem* (1909), gives a clear account of the basis of the Indian desire for protection.

[7] *Report of the Indian Fiscal Commission, 1921-2* (1922). The official summary was published or condensed in newspapers of September 25, 1922.

CHAPTER XIII

[1] C. M. Andrews, *Historical Development of Modern Europe* (1896), p. 101.

[2] For this movement—indeed, for the topics of this chapter generally—reference may be made to C. F. Bastable, *Commerce of Nations*, revised by T. E. Gregory (1923), and A. Viallate, *Economic Imperialism* (1923).

[3] The marks of affinity between protection and Socialism were pointed out by Cavour (*D P.E.*, I, p. 237). For points of resemblance and difference between Mercantilism and Socialism see Hewins, *D.P.E.*, II, p. 727 ; and H. Levy, *Economic Liberalism* (1913), pp. 1–3.

[4] This was illustrated in some of the speeches of Labour members in the recent Preference debate in the House of Commons (1924).

[5] A clear and vigorous account of the movement is given by Ramsay Muir in *The Expansion of Europe*.

[6] J. W. Root, *Colonial Tariffs* (1906), is useful for facts, though to be used cautiously for inferences.

[7] The literature of the campaign is voluminous. I may note simply W. J. Ashley, *The Tariff Problem* (1903 ; 4th ed., 1920), and W. Cunningham, *The Case Against Free Trade* (1911), on the one side, and A. C. Pigou, *The Riddle of the Tariff* (1903), and *Protective and Preferential Import Duties* (1906), on the other.

[8] See quotation in W. J. Ashley, *The Tariff Problem* (1920), pp. 30–1.

[9] J. B. Crozier, in *The Wheel of Wealth* (1906), pp. 128–9, 131.

[10] See H. H. O'Farrell, " British and German Export Trade before the War," *E.J.*, XXVI, pp. 161 *sq.*

[11] On all these questions of comparison the chapters on the industrial leadership of Britain, France, Germany, and the U.S. in Marshall, *Industry and Trade*, should be consulted.

[12] Cp. A. E. Zimmern, *Nationality and Government*, (1919),

pp. 309 *sq.*; Ramsay Muir, *Expansion of Europe* (1922), pp. 246 *sq.*

[13] The Bill was passed in face of a manifesto from leading bankers which recalled the Free Trade petition presented to Parliament by the merchants of London " in a time of depression following a great war a hundred years ago " (Bankers' Manifesto, dated May 12, 1921). The progress of the preference and protectionist movement to this point is described in *The Industrial Crisis and British Policy* (Tariff Commission, 1921).

[14] The McKenna duties were removed and preferences were denounced by the last Parliament, but the Preference debates revealed the existence of a small protectionist section of the Labour party in sympathy with the ideas of the Australian Labour party in this connexion, and the result of the last election has raised a new situation.

[15] The Fordney Tariff Bill has been described as the " most amended measure in the history of the American Congress " (*Journal of Commerce*, New York, September 14, 1922). For comments on the Act see F. W Taussig, *Quarterly Journal of Economics*, XXXVII, pp. 1 *sq.*

[16] Cp. P. Mantoux, " The War and the Industrial Revolution," in *History*, N.S., V, pp 15 *sq.*

ADDITIONAL NOTE

P. 94, ll 4–5. With regard to the statement that the new staple, cotton, grew up without any favour from the Crown, it might be objected that the " infant " industry was protected by the statutory prohibition of Indian cotton goods which obtained, in a greater or less degree, from 1721 to 1774. But it has to be observed that this prohibition was not established with the object of stimulating cotton manufacture in England. It was the result of pressure from the woollen interests, and was primarily intended to protect them against the competition of cotton wares. Moreover, what is known about the history of the Lancashire cotton industry does not warrant the assumption that this prohibition was a necessary factor in its development

P. 90, ll. 3–4—*for* one . . . lose, *read* one could only gain if and to the extent that the other lost, *and after* of gain *insert*

16

for a nation. P. 90, ll. 1c-12—*delete* Moreover . . . imports.
P. 116, ll. 27–8—*for* the mercantilist doctrine *read* mercantilist
ideas. P. 116, l. 29—*for* in *read* primarily determined.
P. 121, l. 7—*for* observers *read* students. P. 194, ll. 17–20—
for When . . . she *read* During the period from the dissolution
of the company down to recent times, India was compelled
to follow the principles of free trade, ostensibly on the ground
of theory, but really for the benefit of England, and in opposition to the wishes not only of the people but, sometimes, of
the Government of India. She

INDEX

PRINTED BY
JARROLD AND SONS LTD,
NORWICH